THE ECONOMIC IMPACT ON UNDER-DEVELOPED SOCIETIES

Essays on International Investment and Social Change

By S. HERBERT FRANKEL

*Professor of Colonial Economic Affairs
in the University of Oxford*

HARVARD UNIVERSITY PRESS
CAMBRIDGE, MASSACHUSETTS
1955

BY THE SAME AUTHOR

Co-operation and Competition in the Marketing of Maze in South Africa, P. S. King & Son, Ltd., London, 1926.

The Railway Policy of South Africa, Hortors, Limited, Johannesburg, 1928.

Capital Investment in Africa, Oxford University Press, 1938.

First printed August 1953
Reprinted October 1953
Reprinted July 1955

PRINTED IN GREAT BRITAIN

TO MY MOTHER

PREFACE

The essays in this volume are linked together by the basic economic problem which in one way or another underlies all of them : that of the clash between the functional forces of modern industrialism and the rapidly disintegrating indigenous economies of communities governed by forms of social organisation unable to yield the living standards increasingly being demanded by all the peoples of the world. Thus all the essays deal with some aspect of the twin processes of disintegration and re-integration : with the disappearance of old structural economic patterns and the challenging need arising therefrom to find means of forming new wholes of social and economic endeavour.

The economist who investigates these processes finds his path strewn with concepts which are frequently an obstruction rather than an aid to his studies. I have therefore included in Part I of this volume essays which examine the conceptual aspects of the problem, and have grouped those which apply these concepts to Africa in Part II.

With the exceptions mentioned below the essays are reprinted as first published but they have been revised to avoid unnecessary duplication, and I have made minor alterations where necessary.

' *The Concept of Colonization* ' was delivered as an Inaugural Lecture before the University of Oxford and is reprinted by kind permission of the Oxford University Press. The second essay first appeared under the title ' *Some Conceptual Aspects of Technical Change* ' in a symposium published in the International Social Science Bulletin, Volume IV, No. 2, Unesco, 1952, to the editors of which I am grateful for permission to reprint the essay here. The third essay incorporates most of two articles. The first was entitled ' " *Psychic* " *and* "*Accounting*" *Concepts of Income and Welfare* ' and was published in Oxford Economic Papers (New Series), Volume IV, No. 1, February 1952, and is reprinted here with kind permission of the Oxford University Press and the editors of Oxford Economic Papers. The other article on which the

essay is based appeared in Income and Wealth Series III
(Bowes and Bowes, Cambridge) under the title : ' *Concepts
of Income and Welfare in Advanced and Under-developed Societies
with special Reference to Intercomparability of National Income
Aggregates* ' ; I wish to thank the publishers and editors for
permission to reprint portions of this article. Both articles
were originally based on a paper read to the Conference of
the International Association on Income and Wealth held in
Royaumont in 1951.

The fourth essay in this volume was written at the invitation of the International Finance Section of the Department
of Economics and Social Institutions, Princeton University,
and was published in its ' Essays in International Finance '
in May 1952 (No. 14) under the title '*Some Aspects of International Economic Development of Under-developed Territories.*'
It is reprinted by kind permission of the editors of the Series,
and of the Director of the International Finance Section.

' *United Nations Primer for Development* ' first appeared
in the Quarterly Journal of Economics for August 1952 and
I wish to thank the editors and publishers of the Journal for
permission to reprint it here.

' *Whither South Africa* ' was read before the Royal Society
of Arts in 1947 ; it has been revised and the statistics brought
up-to-date. I wish to thank the editors of the Journal of the
Royal Society of Arts for permission to reprint the paper,
which first appeared in Volume XCV of its Proceedings.

The seventh essay ' *Some Aspects of Investment and Economic
Development in the Continent of Africa* ' was read at the first
Round Table Discussion of the International Economic
Association at Monaco in September 1950. An abbreviated
version was published in the International Social Science
Bulletin, Volume III, No. 1, Spring 1951. It is printed here
in full by kind permission of the Director-General of Unesco.

With the exception of the Introductory Note, the eighth
essay consists of two articles entitled ' *The Kongwa Experiment* ' which were published in *The Times* of the 4th and 5th
of October, 1950. These are reprinted by kind permission of
The Times Publishing Company Ltd.

The last essay in this volume ' *Some Reflections on Civilization in Africa* ' was delivered as The Hoernlé Memorial

Lecture before the South African Institute of Race Relations in 1952; it is reprinted here without alteration by kind permission of the Institute.

In conclusion I wish to thank Mr. J. D. Carmichael for much valuable help in the preparation of a number of these essays, Mr. T. P. Soper, my Research Assistant, for helping me to see the volume through the press and Dr. W. J. Busschau and Mr. L. H. Samuels for much valuable advice.

To my wife I am indebted for all the secretarial work involved; without her constant encouragement and help these essays would not have been written.

S.H.F.

Nuffield College, Oxford.
February, 1953.

CONTENTS

ESSAY I

THE CONCEPT OF COLONIZATION

I. INTRODUCTION

AT no previous period in history have such large regions and vast populations found themselves drawn irresistibly into new orbits of economic activity, new spheres of conflicting political influence, and new social ideologies, which, disrupting old habit patterns, leave the peoples of the world bewildered and ill at ease. Mankind is once again on the march driven by the great disintegrating but also formative process of colonization which has always been the handmaid of civilization.

It is more than one hundred years since a Professor of Political Economy in the University of Oxford, Herman Merivale, devoted his attention exclusively to the economic aspects of colonization. Much of what he wrote is naturally no longer of relevance to-day, yet the spirit which inspired his *Lectures on Colonization and Colonies : Delivered before the University of Oxford in* 1839, 1840 *and* 1841[1] was prophetic. He realized that his generation was witnessing the birth of yet another world economy which would dwarf in achievement all those of the past. He recognized the significance of the forces which were knitting together the economies bordering on the Atlantic, and were bursting forth to germinate new economic life across the seas : binding far-flung regions to form a new interdependent economic whole. Europe was its centre : an economic power-house from which great colonizing movements radiated outwards with irrepressible vigour of hope and expectation.

Thus he did not, like others, fail to view the colonial expansion of his time as part of a vast process of change based on the release of the powerful forces of industrialism and scientific discovery. Of these the railway, the steamship, and the telegraph were the heralds in the nineteenth century, just as the conquest of the air and the atom are the harbingers

[1] London, 1861.

B

of a new world struggling to be born in the twentieth. No wonder, therefore, that he grew impatient of the mercantilist terminology and viewpoint which dominated discussion of the basic problems of colonization. He spoke of ' those very narrow views of commercial policy, which have become so inveterate by long indulgence, that even those who are convinced of their futility can scarcely shake off the prejudices produced by them '. He expressed the view that ' we constantly under-rate those commercial benefits which are common to us with all the world. . . . To suit our contracted notions of economical gain to a particular country, the gain in question must be something exclusive and monopolized.'[1]

How right he was! When mankind has struck its tents, and the caravan is moving swiftly towards new horizons, the quarrels of the camp-followers appear in retrospect as sordid as they were unimportant. What matters if one or other of the moving caravan has momentarily snatched the bowl to quench his thirst by too long a draught from the fountain of co-operant human effort, and preened himself the while that guile has gained him a place before his brothers? The caravan as a whole moves on. What matters is that it be not turned back to perish in the wilderness.

Endless debates about colonial tariffs and preferences, about the value to the metropolitan countries of new colonies, about the desirability of abandoning or retaining them, about the value of emigration to or investment in them, look somewhat unreal from the viewpoint of our time. Indeed many were unreal. The unreality arose from the attempts to apply that same stultifying ' Political Arithmetick ' which, a century before, Sir Charles Davenant had defined in such modern terms as to make them sound homely even to our ears :

'A great Statesman,' he wrote, ' by consulting all sort of Men, and by contemplating the universal Posture of the Nation, its Power, Strength, Trade, Wealth and Revenues, in any Council he is to offer, by summing up the Difficulties on either Side, and by computing upon the whole, shall be able to form a sound Judgment, and to give a right Advice : and this is what we mean by Political Arithmetick.'[2]

[1] Op. cit., Lecture VII, p. 188.
[2] Sir Charles Davenant : *Discourses on the Publick Revenues, and on the Trade of England*, London, 1698, Part I, p. 15, quoted by Jacob H. Hollander in ' The Dawn of a Science', Chapter I of *Adam Smith*, 1776–1926, University of Chicago Press, 1928.

Much of this art expresses itself to-day in futile attempts to equilibriate the national profit or loss from economic intercourse in all and sundry economic transactions from the sublime to the ridiculous. Not only in war, but in peace, the mirror of our myth-bound minds throws back a distorted vision. In it the well-being of the peoples of the world seems to depend on national economic battles with our neighbours ; on export drives which force them to accept our wares ; on import restrictions which proclaim our independence of their co-operant efforts ; on the orders of leaders who by a stroke of the mighty legislative pen divert the toil of millions this way and that, allegedly regulating our well-being in accordance with the utterance of the great statistical oracle.

The comparative study of fact and fiction in the process of colonization is illuminating. Only when we look back do we realize how greatly the actual forces at work differed from the political conceptions concerning them, and how trivial were the stratagems by which it was hoped they would be controlled.

For the real organic forces which alter the structure of economic relationships between the peoples of the world, which widen their horizons of beliefs, which stimulate them to new effort, which create new spheres of human action and transplant men and women into a new market-place of space-time, cannot be adequately portrayed in the ledgers of the counting-house or in the balance-sheets of imperialism. The wares in the shop windows of human productivity and illusion change incessantly ; nor can the currencies of human effort which pay for them be expressed in terms of any index number of human happiness.

II. TERMINOLOGICAL CONFUSIONS

It is significant that notwithstanding his wide outlook Merivale was unable to formulate a concept of colonization which was entirely free from those mercantilist and territorial associations which he decried. This terminological confusion was general at the time he wrote. It has persisted to the present day.

In the Introduction to the first edition of his lectures Merivale put forward the following definition :

' I may here mention that throughout these Lectures the term Colony is used in the ancient and proper sense, and not in that which has passed from official into general usage, in which it comprehends every species of foreign possession—military stations, such as Gibraltar and Malta ; conquered districts, possessed by native inhabitants with a very slight admixture of the conquerors, such as Ceylon ; mercantile emporia, such as the factories of European powers on the coast of Africa. By a Colony I understand a territory of which the soil is entirely or principally owned by settlers from the mother country.'[1]

Two points in this definition are noteworthy. First, it excludes what has been called the ' sphere of rule ' as opposed to the ' sphere of settlement '.[2] To-day, of course, we use the word ' colonies ' mainly in the contrary sense to designate areas of rule over indigenous peoples. We exclude from the term areas of settlement, and also other areas if the peoples in them have attained independent political status. The change illustrates the shortcomings of a definition based mainly on political criteria.

Secondly, it defines colonization as a process of territorial expansion outwards from a mother country. Indeed Merivale distinguishes the movement even from that which was involved in the creation of replica—or daughter—societies by the Greeks. 'A Grecian colony', he wrote, ' was always emphatically "a people "; a modern colony is " a territory ".'[3]

His conception of the process is much akin to that of the ' moving frontier '—a notion which played such an important role in the ideology which dominated the occupation of free land in the United States and elsewhere in the nineteenth century. As I have shown elsewhere,[4] the occupation of free land was regarded not only as a means of escape from over-population and other economic and social circumstances, but also carried with it the fallacious implication that when free land is no longer available the further growth of income must

[1] Op. cit., p. xii.
[2] Cf. *Greater Rome and Greater Britain*, p. 151, Sir C. P. Lucas, Oxford, 1912.
[3] Herman Merivale : *Introduction to a Course of Lectures in Colonization and Colonies*, 1839.
[4] Cf. ' World Economic Welfare,' *South African Journal of Economics*, vol. ii, No. 3, September 1943.

necessarily be inhibited. Thus arose the concept of the ' mature economy ' which has had many similarly misleading consequences.

No writer has been able to avoid the identification of colonization with particular forms of territorial expansion or with particular political systems. A colony has been defined by one writer as ' a political dependency, settled or pros- pectively to be settled, to some degree, by the citizens of its dominant state '.[1] The same writer classified colonization according to types of industrial organization or forms of settlement, as ' plantation colonies ' or ' farm colonies ' vary- ing with the geography or climate of special regions. It has been thought of[2] as 'primary colonization ', i.e. the trans- formation of an existing society through political control by another power, as distinct from ' secondary colonization ' which expresses the continued transfer of goods, institutions, and ideas from an old country to a new one. The process has by some been identified with, and by others distinguished from, imperialism. It has been classified as complete when conquest has been followed by the transplanting of economic, legal, and cultural institutions ; or as partial when the political tie with the conqueror has snapped ; and it has been sub- classified as voluntary or purely coercive.[3] All these definitions throw valuable light on some aspects of the many exceedingly complex factors which accompany, or influence, the process of colonization. But to my mind they do not penetrate to the fundamental forces of economic growth which always lie at the root of it. It is to them that it is my purpose to draw attention in this essay.

It may, I think, be said that so far colonization in its purest and classic form has generally been thought of in terms of a movement of peoples outwards from a mother country into empty lands. In these they are pictured as reproducing a replica of the previous culture and organization of the mother society. This idea forms a useful point of departure for our further inquiries.

It is true that the desire to fashion replica societies has

---

[1] A. G. Keller : *Colonization—A Study of the Founding of Societies*, Boston, 1908.
[2] Ibid.
[3] M. J. Bonn : *The Crumbling of Empire*, Allen and Unwin, 1938.

been one of the most powerful factors which, for obvious reasons, has consciously and unconsciously influenced the mind of man, just as, since the dawn of history, tribal migration has been so important in the movement of mankind. Nevertheless, I believe it to be misleading to regard them as the essential features of colonization.

Even if we were to adopt the artificial procedure of leaving out of account all cases of conquest, the idea of colonization as only a form of social or political duplication will be seen to have other limitations.

Apart from the fact that from ancient to modern times the history of colonization is so largely a record of the clash of cultures, such an abstract approach overlooks that no natural environments can be assumed to be in all respects identical, or to remain unchanged ; nor is there reason to believe that the human surround will not alter as one generation succeeds another. However imperceptible, and however slow, change may be, of one thing we can be sure : that any new society will come to differ from the old. No matter with what conscious or unconscious beliefs men set forth, they will build a city different from any their fathers or they themselves foresaw. For in their efforts to mould the environment, and to attain equilibrium with it, men are like painters, who, seeking to transfer on to the canvas the images formed within them, paint differently in terms of the dictates of their medium from what they intended, and perforce complete a picture quite other than ever they imagined. So too the builders of society grow to think and to act differently as their task proceeds, and their children too will be buffeted and moulded by other tempests than any from which their parents might have fondly hoped to shield them. Imperceptibly they also will bend their bodies and their minds to the storms of circumstance, changing their institutions and themselves.

Thus already we find ourselves moving away from the concept of colonization as merely a form of territorial expansion. We begin to see a colony as a social unit in process of transformation.

III. The Expansion of Social Horizons

So far we have had our attention riveted on the new encounter itself and have overlooked the parent society. As long as one pictures the process of colonization as the departure of a group to new uninhabited lands, cut off like perpetual Robinson Crusoes on an island world, it matters little that one should think only of the new and forget the old.

Again there are deep historical reasons why such narrowly circumscribed conceptions of colonization should for long have dominated and must needs still colour men's thought. For the greater part of history men have been so little able to bridge the obstacles to communication, have been so space-bound—so largely dependent on their own unaided efforts in tilling small areas of land to wring from them a meagre subsistence—that their very neighbours lived and struggled in a world apart.

The inherited concepts of space-bound man, however, must not blind us to the fact that in all but very primitive subsistence economies the characteristic feature, and conditioning agency, of colonization has been the mutual intercourse between the older and the new society. Indeed, from one aspect history can be viewed as the creation of a succession of world economies in which the peoples linked within them, under the protecting umbrella of a common system of law and order, and enforceable contracts, were able in varying degrees to escape from their dependence on territorially restricted activities. They established those wider income-producing relations which involved a new dependence of men on each other, be they at one or at the other end of the open world economy of their time.

The limits to an increase in the income of a subsistence producer, or of any productive unit whose relations with the wider world economy of its time remain restricted, are, like the frontiers of his land and mind, soon reached. For more effective action in his continuous probing of the unknown, man requires the co-operant activity of others. Without their help he cannot obtain that wider pattern of experience—in the face of the real and imagined dangers which threaten his life and well-being—which constitutes increased income.

Thus an addition to income implies an expansion of the horizon of individual and social experience. It implies that a subsistence economy, or indeed any microcosmic unit of economic activity, can only escape from territorial, customary, or other limits to its structural growth by integration within a greater whole. In this way men throw off their dependence on a restricted environment to which they have become habituated. They come to rely increasingly on the success with which others create income elsewhere.

This process of emancipation from the bonds of space, as I have suggested on another occasion,[1] is paralleled by a similar process of institutional change which releases man from the bonds of time. In a subsistence economy men cannot ensure a flow of future income otherwise than through the limited possibilities which can be attained by storing up stocks of commodities. To ensure an expansion of future income men must make those changes in their social relations, and form those new personal bonds, which will enable them to make use of, and hence cause them to become dependent on, the income-creating activities of others who can be trusted to make available—in exchange for present benefits—a flow of income in the future. Just as the bursting of customary or physical frontiers releases man from the bonds of space, so too the creation of debt releases him from the bonds of time, and can be regarded as a forcing-house of civilization.

The production of income, in the wider economy of time and space, rests neither on the parochial power of a tribal unit nor on the political powers of a national state. Neither the one nor the other can achieve the maximum well-being, or release to the full the potential powers of its members, by imposing its stamp upon them.

This digression enables us to widen further the concept of colonization. It becomes clear that, as colonization proceeds, it changes continuously not only the surround to which the new colony must adapt itself but also that within which the parent community must henceforth function, and to which, if it is to survive, it must constantly attune itself.

We must cease to look upon colonization as either a

---

[1] 'World Economic Solidarity,' *South African Journal of Economics*, vol. x, No. 3, September 1942.

mere outward or as a one-way movement. The process is reciprocal. That is one of its most significant characteristics.

The present economic plight of Europe is a grim illustration of this fact. For a whole generation before the outbreak of the First World War, Europeans came to believe in the inevitable continuance of European economic and cultural domination over the then peripheral regions of their world economy. All the forces of change appeared to them to radiate only outwards from the metropolitan centres of Western civilization. They paid but little conscious attention to the fact that Europe's strength was based on the continuous adaptation, and re-adaptation, of the then economically united intra-European economy to the demands of the newly emerging and greater whole. They even overlooked that the capital which they were accumulating, at a rate never previously surpassed, which made them the bankers of the world, was derived from that ever-lengthening chain of slowly evolving co-operant activity which spanned the world. This it was which enabled them, by drawing on ever new natural resources, to reduce the cost of their accustomed livelihood and to accumulate that surplus.

Thus Europe itself became a specialized sector of the Western world economy. In Europe's growing dependence upon it she could ill afford to rend those delicate bonds of human co-operation which now, after two world wars, lie torn and tattered at her feet.

The history of all the world economies of the past—of Greece and Rome, of Spain and Portugal—illustrates this process of integration while the world economy was expanding, and of decay when new structural inventiveness declined.

For the human bonds of economic and social cohesion take longer to fashion than the making of mechanical devices, and they are far more delicate and vulnerable. Education and reason are not enough to bring them to birth. They depend on mutual trust and loyalty, and on the slowly garnered experience of men ripened in judgment and steeled in character by the trial and tribulation of time.

It is possible that the flush of scientific and mechanical success has blinded our European civilization to that deeper social contribution of every civilized man which rests on his unique propensity to form with others ever new partnerships of joint endeavour if he be given a favourable climate of law and order to ensure their growth. This fashioning of human links is a humble role which any man can play. Yet it is a more powerful generator of human achievement than any machine which man has yet devised.

For the mechanistic climate of our time causes us to forget that not only man but also the machine dies soon. As Professor Hayek has so rightly stressed, ' the essential characteristic of capital . . . is that it needs replacement. . . . The important thing is not that the capital has been produced but that it (or some equivalent) has to be reproduced.'[1] That process of reproduction involves the maintenance of an existing, or the creation of a new, chain of human relationships to harness the gifts of nature.

We as yet know very little concerning the nature of the organic forces which further, and the obstacles to them which prevent, the timely adaptation of existing structural patterns to a new environmental surround. In the long history of colonization there has been but little comparative analysis of the factors which made possible, or prevented, the successful integration of metropolitan societies within the larger economies to which they gave birth.

Such inquiries into the nature of economic adaptability, and the significance of social mobility, should, I believe, form the basis of economic studies in the field of colonization. They can throw much-needed light not only on the causes of the rise and decline of civilizations but also on the problems of all under-developed societies. Our generation has witnessed all the horrors of destruction and disintegration. It now requires new knowledge, and new faith born thereof, concerning the healing forces of reintegration. To these history, fortunately, also bears witness. The great psychological stresses which are reflected in the racial and class conflicts of our time are frequently symptoms of that same lack of continuous adjustment between old and newly emerging structures of activity. Where the adjustment is not mutual it leads to unfreedom : with its accompanying feelings of frustration in the new and corresponding feelings of guilt in the old

[1] F. A. Hayek: *The Pure Theory of Capital*, pp. 87-8, London, 1941.

society. This psychological *malaise* arrests the unfolding of human capacity. It leads finally to attempts to solve structural disharmonies by an appeal to force.

IV. STRUCTURAL EVOLUTION

It remains for us to take the final step in our analysis. We must probe below the popularly entrenched terminology which differentiates unduly between the problems of economic development in parent and in daughter societies, in metropolitan and in colonial countries, in so-called developed and in so-called under-developed areas of the world. We must concentrate our attention on the basic forces of change which are common to them all.

I submit that if we look below the surface of immediate circumstance we find that colonization is nothing more or less than the process of macrocosmic and microcosmic social and economic growth itself; that the forces which produce or arrest change in any society or social structure, old or new, spring from a common genus, and give rise to problems which are met with in varying degree in all cases of economic and social development. In every society the process of economic and social growth rests upon the emergence of new economic and social structures. These incorporate new patterns of personal relationships, new habits which co-ordinate the actions of individuals for the attainment of other ends—even if those ends be but dimly comprehended by the individuals linked together in the new productive structure.

Colonization is the process by which such new structures are evolved. It implies the withdrawal of individuals from established structural patterns to found a new colony of endeavour within, and in relation to, the changing natural or human surround. The later structural forms react on the former, and may lead eventually to their complete dissolution. But, let me emphasize again, the process, like all growth, takes time. Each of these life-giving forces of structural development has its own time-scale which men can disregard only at their peril. Mechanistic devices which quicken the pace unduly in one direction will but destroy those deeper mutual harmonies of man *in* nature to which alone she will yield her blessings.

In the growth of a new industry, even in a highly industrialized and complex modern economy, we see the withdrawal of individuals from other industries and their regroup-
ing to form a new pattern, a new cell, a new colony of activity.
Those who initiated such movements, who, each in his own
way, developed modern industry and commerce, who from
such small colonies and cells of association with others
fashioned structures which grew into specialized systems of
co-operation, harnessing the work of unknown thousands
throughout the world, were colonizers.

It is perhaps no exaggeration to say that all social and
economic growth is initiated by individuals, pioneering their
way towards the creation of a new social group, whether it
be to develop a new school of painting, of architecture, of the
religious life, of education, or of science. Everywhere the
process commences with the colonizing activities of the few.
These gradually extend their newly invented pattern of
thought and action to attune the minds of the many to a new
productive harmony. If it be founded on freedom, and its
inherent plasticity be not made sterile by the deadening hand
of regimentation or spoliation, it will enable yet others fearlessly to undertake the ungrateful tasks of change.

The great modern movements of agricultural and consumers' co-operation and communal settlement, the new
agencies for the reclamation of the land, for the collective
prevention of illness and disease, for the rehabilitation of the
injured, and for vaster projects like the re-colonization of
neglected regions, on the model of the great experiments in
decentralization of the Tennessee Valley Authority—to
mention only a few—fall into the same category, and illustrate
man's structural inventiveness.

Indeed one of the immeasurable, but for that reason
certainly not less important, constituents of income may well
be this propensity of individuals to value highly, and for its
own sake, the possibility of association, in however humble a
capacity, with the process of birth, growth, and survival, of
particular patterns and structures of activity. Indeed, at
times, the deep-seated emotional and other imponderable
feelings of fulfilment and security which these associations
yield are so strong that they cause men to cling too long to

patterns which are no longer economical in terms of the changing surround.

The point, however, to which I would like to return is that this process of economic growth cannot be thought of in terms of any one single nation or state acting as a whole. What we call a nation is but a symbolic expression for a society which harbours within it innumerable social structures, which are linked directly and indirectly to complementary structures in other societies throughout the world economy of its time. The African who works in a copper mine in Northern Rhodesia achieves a higher standard of income than his brother in the African bush because he happens to have been drawn into a new colony of human activity—the copper-mining industry. But the focal point of that colony of modern effort lies neither in Northern Rhodesia nor in Africa. It may at one time be found in Europe—at another in America.

When the hum of activity for markets far and near has been throttled in a coal-mining area by technical or economic changes over which that particular community of producers has no control, a new process of colonization is required. This will attract men away from the area, or bring other co-operant factors of production into it to form a new pattern of activity. So too a group of income producers in the Far East, having subdued a difficult environment with the aid of modern science to produce a specialized raw material required by the world economy, may be confronted by a technical discovery which enables a similar product to be produced synthetically elsewhere. Once again a new process of colon-ization—of structural change—has to be initiated.

Thus at no point can any colony of economic activity, which is directly or indirectly linked to the economy of the modern world, sever itself from the income stream of that greater whole from which it draws its nutriment and to which it makes its contribution. At no point can any single cell or structure shirk the burdens of change which co-operation with others involves. At no point can it permit itself to be frozen into rigidity—unless it be to court destruction through dissolution into its constituent parts, and, by thus perishing, to assume what A. N. Whitehead, writing in this sense of the decline and fall of the Roman

Republic, called 'a new function in the process of generation.'[1]

This seed-bed of change must not be viewed in narrow materialistic terms. Economic growth implies a new synthesis between man's thought and action in relation to the natural resources of the globe. That new synthesis develops new personalities in the sense of individuals bound to each other by new loyalties and social relationships.

'I would like to meet the ethnographer who could accomplish the task,' wrote Professor Malinowski, ' of sorting out a westernized African into his component parts without destroying the one thing in him which matters—his personality. The educated African is a new type of human being, endowed with abilities and energies, with advantages and handicaps, with problems and visions, which neither his European neighbour nor his ' blanket ' brother are heirs to.'[2]

In making use of this quotation I do not want to join issue with my friends the anthropologists as to whether such a westernized African can be classified according to the usages of their science. I merely wish to use this as an example to emphasize that at the root of all true social growth lies the unfolding of personality itself. The development of personality in turn involves that widening of the horizon of human relationships to which I have referred. Thus it follows, as Malinowski also stressed, ' that the whole concept of European culture '—or, I would add, of any culture—' as a cornucopia from which things are freely given is misleading '.[3] The receiver and the giver are as closely linked as the master and the slave ; neither can escape the implications of their mutual relationship. Nor can the exceedingly diverse forces which give rise to colonization, or economic growth, be set in motion by any single society, nation, or collective will. For they result from those innumerable, and as yet dimly comprehended, agencies which lie embedded in society itself.

That is why so large a part of colonization is unconscious. Men carry with them throughout their lives not only the habit patterns of their youth but the memory patterns of the

[1] A. N. Whitehead : *Adventures of Ideas*, p. 375, Cambridge University Press, 1933.
[2] Bronislaw Malinowski : *The Dynamics of Culture Change—An Inquiry Into Race Relations in Africa*, edited by Phyllis M. Kaberry, New Haven, Yale University Press, Humphrey Milford, Oxford University Press, 1945, p. 25.
[3] Ibid.

society of which they form a part, and whose heritage has formed them. That also is why no nation or society can know in advance the direction of its own growth, and still less can it know the influence it will exert upon other nations or societies.

It might be contended by some that the modern colonial policies of European Powers—just because they are so concerned to further the welfare of colonial peoples—must necessarily be excepted from this view. I doubt the validity of this contention. The Spanish and the Portuguese, and innumerable other colonizing Powers, in ancient and modern times, have left a record strewn with no less clearly defined, though different, aims. Yet that which finally evoked the process of growth by mimesis, by compulsion, by persuasion, or by perhaps the strongest of them all—migration, and which brought to fruition a new world of life and action in their colonial territories, bore little relation to the erstwhile plans of their thinkers, politicians, or administrators.

V. CONCLUSION

It is against this background that I submit we must pursue our studies of the unfolding relations between the less and more advanced economies of the modern world.

Let me give just one example of such studies, which might be called the dilemma of Trusteeship.

The modern concept of Trusteeship grew out of that great humanitarian movement based on a common Jewish and Christian heritage which, to their undying credit, the British people brought to practical fruition in the abolition of slavery. It was based on the desire to protect weaker peoples against misuse by the stronger. It aimed at preventing those abuses which always accompany the unfettered and corrupting use of absolute power.

But Trusteeship implies the existence of Trustees. Where, we must ask, is there to be found that body or nation of philosopher kings which, endowed with the gifts of prophecy, knows not only who must change and who shall remain unchanged, what shall be born and what shall remain unborn, but possesses also that most precious gift of heaven—the ability to change itself ?

For it follows from my previous analysis that Trusteeship must involve a two-way process : both the guardian and the ward must change. Even if a nation of Trustees could be found which possesses the power, and the knowledge, to mould men—for their own good—nearer to its prophetic vision, it would still have to escape from those conscious and unconscious rigidities in its own way of life and thought, which prevent it undergoing those changes which alone can ensure the maintenance of its economic power, and its own survival.

I believe that the time has come for a new assessment of the problems of development of the backward regions of the world. For that purpose I suggest we must view civilization not as something which any society or nation has finally perfected, and can hold in trust until others are able to make use of it, but as an ever-uncompleted task.[1] This all men must ever take upon themselves anew, shirking no sacrifice and effort in its burdensome pursuit. Is it not possible that the European Trustee Powers have themselves become entangled in a rigid structural pattern of the past? In Europe itself many of the life-giving springs of economic unity and harmony have dried up, and its circumscribed idolatries distintegrate the framework of cohesion both in the West and in the East.

The colonies and under-developed areas of the free world await reintegration into yet another, and greater, world economy which will give shelter once again to the emergence of new co-operant units of human endeavour irrespective of race, colour, and creed. Europe itself must also merge into that wider sphere of action and of hope. The Trustees must consciously subject themselves to those changes which time dictates, if they are to inspire constructive change in others.

Above all let us beware of unconsciously corrupting established concepts to serve the expediencies of the day. The present tendency to identify Trusteeship with the creation of the Colonial Welfare State, in which the government is regarded as the sole impulse to social and economic growth, may well be found to be but the reflection of powerful current

---

[1] This view is further developed in the last essay in this volume.

ideologies which obscure the deeper factors in economic evolution.

May I remind you of that trenchant judgment of de Tocqueville:

'The physiognomy of a government may best be judged in its colonies, for there its features are magnified and rendered more conspicuous. When I wish to study the merits and faults of the administration of Louis XIV, I must go to Canada; its deformity is there seen as through a microscope.'

It is not only the merits and faults of governments, but of whole civilizations in process of growth and decay, that are mirrored and magnified in the societies which fall under the sway of their thought and deeds.

There is need for a new approach to the problem of social and economic growth by students, who, I trust, will be prepared to re-examine these comparative problems of economic evolution. Only thus can we hope to discover afresh the forces which cause men to form those new productive relationships, which will rescue them from tribal and national isolation, from the false security of tribal custom and the equally false security of national power, and from ignorant and too narrowly confined dependence on the immediate environment of nature and of man. Thus may they build a new hope and a new faith in man himself.

'In what way, therefore,' inquired Adam Smith, 'has the policy of Europe contributed either to the first establishment, or to the present grandeur of the colonies of America? In one way, and in one way only, it has contributed a good deal. *Magna virum Mater!* It bred and formed the men who were capable of achieving such great actions, and of laying the foundation of so great an empire; ... The colonies owe to the policy of Europe the education and great views of their active and enterprising founders; and some of the greatest and most important of them, so far as concerns their internal government, owe to it scarce anything else.'[1]

[1] *The Wealth of Nations*, Book 4, Chapter VII, Part II.

C

ESSAY II

SOME ASPECTS OF TECHNICAL CHANGE

I. DEFINITIONS

WHEN I was privileged to receive an invitation to contribute this article to a symposium on ' Social Implications of Technical Change ' I hesitated for some time before accepting it. I wanted to try to define more clearly in my own mind the problem involved, and the contribution which an economist might make to a discussion of it at the present time.

I came to the conclusion that perhaps the most useful approach would be to examine some of the conceptual ideas which, consciously or unconsciously, provide the framework of controversy in this field of study. In doing so, I shall not confine myself to any particular stage of economic development, or any particular region, except for purposes of illustration.

As a starting-point it may be useful to draw attention to certain semantic peculiarities which, I think, are in themselves indicative both of the present climate of opinion, and of some confusions which seem worthy of further examination.

The first of these semantic, or definitional, peculiarities is the fact that we so readily tend to speak of ' the social consequences of technical change ', and not of ' technical change as a social consequence '. This is very significant. It shows that we have formed the habit of regarding technical change in mechanistic terms—as an independent force, which, by impinging on society, sets in motion certain desirable, or undesirable, reactions. These reactions, since they are regarded as the inevitable consequence of the external force, are then presumed to require study in the same fatalistic spirit in which one might try to cope with the destruction left in the wake of a battle or of an earthquake.

A parallel can be drawn between the use of the term ' the Industrial Revolution ', with its undertones of cataclysmic suddenness and consequences, and the frequent implication that technical change necessarily takes a similar form, and shatters all around it. But, as an eminent contemporary economic historian[1] has reminded us : ' the changes . . . spoken of as the Industrial Revolution . . . were not merely " industrial " but also social and intellectual. . . . The word " revolution " implies a suddenness of change that is not in fact characteristic of economic processes '. He remarks that ' the phrase Industrial Revolution has . . . become so firmly embedded in common speech that it would be pedantic to offer a substitute '. Let us hope that the term technical change is not yet as inseparable from its present narrow mechanistic connotation.

The Oxford Dictionary defines technique as the ' manner of artistic execution or performance ' and the word technical as ' belonging or relating to an art or arts '. None of these (or other available) definitions indicates the presence of any exogenous forces affecting the work of individuals concerned with changing techniques. On the contrary, they refer to the ways in which certain activities are conducted. But as Professor Oakeshott has emphasized in his Inaugural Lecture on Political Education to ' understand an activity *is to know it as a concrete whole* ; *it is to recognize the activity as having the source of its movement within itself* (Italics not in the original). An understanding which leaves the activity in debt to something outside itself is, for that reason, an inadequate understanding. And if political activity is impossible without a certain kind of knowledge and a certain sort of education, then this knowledge and education are not mere appendages to the activity but are part of the activity itself and must be incorporated in our understanding of it.'[2]

II. Knowing and Doing

In the same way, I submit, it is important to recognize that an activity (or performance) which, for convenience, we describe as technical, does not consist as it were of two parts, namely of (*a*) knowing how to do a thing, and of (*b*) doing it. It consists essentially of one process as a whole : the conducting of the activity itself. This can be illustrated by the

---

[1] Professor T. S. Ashton : *Industrial Revolution* 1760–1830, Oxford University Press, 1948.
[2] *Political Education*. An Inaugural Lecture by Professor Michael Oakeshott. Bowes and Bowes, Cambridge, 1951.

arrestingly simple example which Professor Oakeshott has used in support of his thesis that ' political activity comes first and a political ideology follows after '. He takes the example of cookery : ' It might be supposed that an ignorant man, some edible materials, and a cookery book compose together the necessities of a self-moved activity called cooking. But nothing is further from the truth. The cookery book is not an independently generated beginning from which cooking can spring ; it is nothing more than an abstract of somebody's knowledge of how to cook : it is the stepchild, not the parent of the activity. The book, in its turn, may help to set a man on to dressing a dinner, but if it were his sole guide he could never, in fact, begin : the book speaks only to those who know already the kind of thing to expect from it and consequently how to interpret it.

' Now, just as a cookery book presupposes somebody who knows how to cook, and its use presupposes somebody who already knows how to use it, and just as a scientific hypothesis springs from a knowledge of how to conduct a scientific investigation, and separated from that knowledge is powerless to set empiricism to work, so a political ideology must be understood, not as an independently premeditated beginning for political activity, but as knowledge (in an abstracted and generalized form) of a traditional manner of attending to the arrangements of a society. The catechism which sets out the purposes to be pursued merely abridges a concrete manner of behaviour in which those purposes are already hidden.'

Similarly, if we are to speak meaningfully of the effects of technical change we must, I suggest, be very careful to avoid falling into the common, and facile, error of thinking that changes in knowing how to do a certain thing can be separated from changes in the actual doing of it. This is the type of error which is frequently introduced when we speak of making available to a backward society the ' know-how ' of a new technical process : we are not making available two processes, namely, a mental process of abstract technical knowledge on the one hand, and of the actual performance on the other. We are speaking only of the one process—the performance itself. The idea that technical change is somehow an exogenous force altering the established day-to-day activities of society springs, I suggest, from this erroneous way of speaking and thinking. It consists in the fallacious belief that a society's activities proceed in two separate compartments : the first containing the process of abstract willing or knowing, the other containing the application of such willing or knowing. It is on the basis of a similarly erroneous conception of the nature of economic activity that we so readily conclude that technical change is a kind of abstract force which has certain social consequences, and fail to see that what we describe as the consequences of this imaginary force is simply part and parcel of the activity itself. When, for example, there is a change from farming to coal mining, this will involve the development of new aptitudes and new habits of work over a wide range of new economic and social activities. The change will not be completed until it has resulted in a community all of whose activities (and not only those directly related to the production of coal) have been rearranged or have grown into a new pattern of life and work. If now we regard the introduction of coal mining as a purely mechanical process, which will have certain social consequences, we fail to see that what we regard as the result or consequence, is but the continuous, and necessarily uneven, process of change itself. Thus, if the workers in the coal mine are inadequately housed, or suffer deficiencies in the standard of nutrition, education, or recreation now necessary in their new environment, these are not the consequence of the process of change to coal mining, but rather of a failure to complete it. Even the direct activity of extracting coal cannot be brought to optimum efficiency unless all the other economic and social activities to which that task must be related, and with which it must be integrated, have been developed. Indeed, coal mining cannot even begin until some change in the previous aptitudes, habits, and patterns of social organization have taken place.

Let us examine, for the sake of illustration, a highly simplified example of what, presumably, would nowadays be regarded merely as a technical change. Let us assume that it is desired to increase the productivity of a subsistence cattle-owning African community which has never engaged in the production of butter or cheese, either for sale or for its own consumption. It is hoped not only to get this community to consume these products itself, but also to market some of them so as to enable the society to increase its income by selling the surplus dairy produce, and buying other goods with the money so obtained.

III.   PREREQUISITES OF TECHNICAL CHANGE

At first sight the problem might appear to be merely one of introducing new methods of production, and the instruments, tools or machines appropriate thereto.   But what is really involved is a vast change in social beliefs and practices —if, that is, it be assumed that the society in question is to remain intact as a society—an assumption which, as we shall see, raises questions of quite another kind. Here, for the moment, let us consider only what far-reaching social changes will have to be made to enable technical change—which we nowadays so readily tend to abstract as the prime mover— to be introduced at all. The utilization of cattle as a source of income in a monetary and accounting sense presupposes a basic alteration in the economic structure of the society.   It presupposes not only the introduction of money, but a complete re-casting of the traditional values of the community. Thus it presupposes a change in the system of land ownership and use; in the laws and conventions governing access to land, and in the traditional beliefs as to how, and by whom, it is to be cultivated—whether by men or by women, by individuals working for themselves or for others.   Moreover it presupposes an aptitude, ability, and willingness to tolerate, recognize, and provide for the emergence and training of groups in the community which are not attached to the land at all. This, in turn, presupposes the growth of new aptitudes and patterns of behaviour which will regulate their social and mutual relations not in accordance with the customs suited to shifting subsistence cultivation, roaming cattle herds, and the thrill of the chase, but to those of a settled agricultural and urban population.   There is presupposed, therefore, the parallel emergence of a group of persons concerned not only with dairy production itself but with the transport, distribution, marketing and finance of all that the new producers have to buy and all they have to sell. These, however, necessitate a political structure—local, provincial, national and trans-national—suited to the establishment of these complementary economic, scientific and financial activities ; they presuppose therefore the willingness, aptitude and ability of the community to permit, and, indeed, to pro- mote the growth of all the legal, political and administrative institutions necessary to harmonize the rights and duties of the persons engaged in this new complex inter-dependent economy.

The purpose of this long list of social adjustments is to show that whatever it be that we may care to designate as technical change, it is but one aspect of mutually determined, and determining, processes of growth on many fronts of the social structure as a whole. It is idle to endeavour to ascertain which change is the innovation or cause, and which is the effect. For when we designate one change as cause and another as effect, we are but examining the process of change itself from different points of observation.

The attempt to establish particular absolute causes of change is misleading, for it misconceives the very nature of the process of change or growth itself.

Let me revert again to that commonplace view of technical change which regards it as resulting from the application of new knowledge—of technical ‘ know-how ’. Such a view presupposes a kind of mental certainty as to the change which is required in order to bring about a particular conse- quence in the near or distant future. Basic to this way of thinking is the implicit assumption that the ‘ know-how ’ exists, as it were, as a stock of techniques—like a stock of raw materials—which can be drawn upon at will, and applied to any situation, in order to produce the desired, and therefore foreseeable, end. It is because we tend to think in such abstract terms that we are led to imagine that somehow economic development, or the lack of it, can be explained in terms of the presence or absence of adequate quantities of factors of production ; as when it is suggested that all that is required to assist the development of backward societies is to give to or lend to them part of the world’s accumulated technical knowledge and capital—just as one might give an injection to a patient to cure him.

This way of speaking is based on a profound misconception : technical knowledge, the machine and capital goods in general never exist in the abstract but always only in the relatively fleeting form suited to the momentary situation, and to that complex of unique problems to which they have been adapted. They have no power independent of the performance of which they are capable. They are the expression of man's response to the changing problems set by the environment and by his fellow men. When the problems which constitute man's framework of reference change, they become useless. That is why they cannot be readily transferred from one situation to another. For meeting any new situation, new thoughts, new aptitudes, new action will be required. But knowledge has to grow ; capital has to be created afresh on the basis of continuous experiment ; and new hopes and beliefs have to evolve to urge men and women forward—for in the last resort they alone are the carriers alike of past experience, and of new endeavour. It is because all these new activities are not independent of the existing institutions into which they have to be fitted, and which have in turn to be adjusted to them, that the process of change is so complex and—if it is to proceed harmoniously —necessarily so slow.

IV. DISCONTINUOUS CHANGES

It is the attempt to simplify that process, to avoid the gradualness of change in order to pluck the quick fruits of endeavour in one direction—at the expense of inactivity in others—which accounts for social maladjustments. In a society in which all changes were to take place at rates so well adjusted to each other as not to disturb the basic harmony and integration of its constituent parts, there would be no social consequences of change but only harmonious change itself. When, however, rates of change are very discontinuous it may well happen that one sector of the society cannot be meaningfully integrated into the social life of the community at all—so that, as far as that sector is concerned, society as a whole no longer exists.

The most extreme case of failure to achieve a balanced

rate of change is that of slavery. It illustrates in its most terrible form the deliberate disintegration of established patterns of social and human values in order to pursue an immediate objective. Slavery not only detaches men and women by force from an established pattern of social relationships but, by using them as chattels for the ends of others, denies them both the opportunity to reconstruct a new society for themselves, and the right to become an integrated meaningful part of the society of their masters. In a society based on slavery the uneasy and unstable rule of force takes the place of that social harmony necessary for the full development of each part of the disrupted whole.

Slavery is an extreme case of the establishment of new structural patterns which by their very nature prevent further economic and social growth. But there have been, and continue to be, many less extreme, yet parallel, situations.

The large movements of indentured labour during the nineteenth century—like the migration of some recruited labour in Africa to-day—illustrate the consequences of attempts to use labour in pursuance of an immediate objective without considering the need to integrate the individuals concerned into a new meaningful social pattern.

In South Africa, for example, the need to obtain Indian labour for the Natal sugar industry arose because it was not possible to detach Africans for that purpose from their own indigenous society. The structure of the sugar industry was thus established on the basis of Indian unskilled labour, and the Indians were forced to remain separated from both the European and the African social structures. This not only inhibited the evolution of a meaningful society for Indians in South Africa, but also froze the economic pattern of the sugar industry itself. The whole economic evolution of Natal was retarded by the failure to establish the Indian immigrant as a creative part of South African society.

I suggest that when we view the problems of change in the light of these considerations we shall accustom ourselves to focus our studies, to a greater extent than heretofore, on the historical evolution of the structural patterns of developing societies. By so doing we shall, I believe, be able to place the emphasis in studies of change where it belongs : on the need to discover to what extent rates of change in different parts of the society are moving towards, or diverging from, that minimum degree of social and psychological harmony necessary for its maintenance or evolution.

In using these terms I am aware of the fact that I am begging many questions. However, what I have in mind is something far simpler than the necessarily vague terminology I have used may at first sight indicate.

To illustrate this let me again refer to the lessons of the Industrial Revolution and quote again from Professor Ashton's valuable judgment : ' Experience has taught us,' he writes, ' that an industrial society needs a framework of public services if it is to operate without social discomfort. . . . With the best will in the world, the transition from farms and cottages to factories and cities could never have been smooth. If the legislative machine had turned out statutes with the same speed as the mules turned out yarn there would still have been social disorder. For much of the overcrowding and squalor was the result of the fact that progress in science was then, as to-day, more rapid than in administration. "The remote influence of arrangements has been somewhat neglected," wrote Dr. Kay in 1832, adding to this meiosis that the neglect arose "not from the want of humanity, but from the pressure of occupation and the deficiency of time." . . . Not until the whole apparatus of government had been drastically reformed and a body of qualified public servants had been called into being could life in urban areas be other than squalid. If the industrial revolution was not able to bring its rewards in full measure to the ordinary man and woman it is to the defects of administrative, and not of economic processes, that the failure must be ascribed.'

V.   CONCLUSION

What, I suggest, is most required now, in relation to the thought and practice of our predecessors, is a new awareness, not only of the need to adapt administrative and social arrangements to the pressure of economic and political events, but also of the fact that the political and economic pressures themselves so largely depend on those arrangements. Thus we should envisage neither the pressure of technical, nor those of political happenings as accidental, in the sense that they are independent causes of our problems. Instead we should accustom ourselves to see them as mutually inter-dependent processes. For that reason we must discipline ourselves to examine them everywhere in sufficient detail to lay bare their mutual relations. By so doing we may perhaps hope to quicken that sense of social inventiveness and responsibility which makes change not a burden, but an adventure in the art of government and mutual adaptation in free societies. For the sting of change lies not in change itself but in change which is devoid of social meaning.

Let me conclude with a final example. All over Africa, and, indeed, in many parts of the under-developed world, erstwhile members of simple rural economies find themselves drawn into urban centres of industry. For many of these men and women these centres are only the places in which they work; their social self remains located with their families, which are still eking out a precarious livelihood in rural conditions as yet unadapted to modern forms of production, or to the basic needs of health, education and the like. Even when these families come to the towns they find themselves psychologically and socially ill-equipped to establish satisfactory patterns of living there. Yet we know little so far about the administrative arrangements which must be evolved to cope with the changing activities of these wanderers in the twilight of newly emerging social structures. Very few detailed studies of their thinking and their needs exist ; fewer still of their psychological reactions, and least of all of the ways and means of emancipating them to grapple with their problems by that most basic form of all political education—the conscious sharing in the governance of affairs by trial and error.

We know little of the processes involved in the vast change of aptitudes which these developments require, of the time they take, and the obstacles they encounter. There is need of carefully documented comparative studies of them in different regions. Moreover, only experience, and a knowledge which exhibits clearly the full burden of change, can prevent needlessly hasty development in this or that direction. All too often a socially uneconomic development is embarked upon because those who initiate it are unaware of its cost, or not responsible for its unavoidable accompanying economic and social changes. But change which is not in harmony with the social resources and needs of a community may well prove to be not a blessing but a curse.

It is here that the economist can be of help in examining the relative individual and social costs and benefits of alternative choices, and in disentangling the real from the apparent expected effects of the fiscal and economic burdens involved.

ESSAY III

CONCEPTS OF INCOME AND WELFARE
AND THE INTERCOMPARABILITY OF
NATIONAL INCOME AGGREGATES

I. INTRODUCTION

IN this essay I propose to discuss certain conceptual problems concerning the meaning of income and product in under-developed countries which have confronted investigators endeavouring to compare national income aggregates of advanced societies with similar calculations attempted for so-called under-developed or pre-industrial communities. The same problem arises, as I myself have found in the course of making official estimates of the National Income of South Africa, in trying to arrive at a satisfactory meaning for income aggregates calculated for a society like South Africa which incorporates so greatly differing ' economies ' as that of the indigenous peoples of the country on the one hand, and that of the modern economic sector on the other.

At the outset I wish to record the benefit I have received from the work of Professor Simon Kuznets on this question, particularly from his valuable paper on ' National Income and Industrial Structure.'[1] This paper exhibits the impasse which confronts national income calculators when they endeavour to compare income aggregates for developed and under-developed societies—or as Professor Kuznets calls them, ' industrial and pre-industrial ' countries ; by which he denotes, ' on the one hand, an economy dominated by business enterprises, using advanced industrial techniques and ordinarily with a large proportion of its population in large cities ; and, on the other hand, an economy in which a large part of production is within the family and rural community, a minor share of resources is devoted to advanced industrial production and a minor part of its population lives in cities.'

The crux of the difficulty of definition arises from the

---

[1] Read before the Washington Meeting of the Econometric Society in September 1947 ; *Econometrica*, Volume 17 Supplement, July, 1949.

fact that as between, *and even within*, developed and under-developed societies there are great differences in the range of activities to which a *highly refined accounting concept of income* can be applied.

The difficulty with which I am here concerned arises, not merely as a result of different technical methods of organizing production, for example, in business enterprises and market economies as opposed to authoritarian, family or subsistence economies, but has its origin rather in the different objectives and ideals which consciously or unconsciously dominate the communities whose individual and social economic activities are being compared. In the last resort it is these historical and traditional factors, and not merely the state of technique and organization, which are the basic cause of differences in the nature and form of the ' income ' produced by them.

To anyone who has had experience of economically less advanced communities, in which fundamental social factors often reveal themselves more directly and forcefully than they do in more complex societies, it is clear that at all times the attempt by the individual to obtain what we call ' income ' is an attempt to achieve a social purpose and is not an isolated activity. It is not merely (and sometimes not at all) an attempt to create a set of individual values or an abstract entity such as ' an individual income stream '. The creation of ' income ' is of a piece with social communication—even if the accounting or economic symbolism which we employ in more advanced societies is such as to disguise this fact. What ' income ' is, and how it is valued, is determined by the society in which the individual finds himself. The ' creation ' of income is not the solo act of a Robinson Crusoe marooned on an island. Even Robinson Crusoe did not act merely according to the dictates of his ' natural ' appetites : he brought with him from the society to which he belonged not only a stock of goods but, far more important, a set of values, ideals, and objectives.

Our actions are not solely determined in isolation : they depend also on the influence we wish to exert upon others, and which their activities in turn exert upon us. Just as economic production depends on social co-operation, so the symbolism according to which it is regulated is socially determined.

To take an imaginary example; in a community of absolute pagans, he that wishes to build a temple to the deity would be engaged upon a social act of persuasion, and he could not engage upon it unless his views had gained sufficient acceptance to bring about social co-operation; therefore to pursue an ideal in isolation is to cut oneself off from the community and from social life. The ' satisfaction ' derived from an individual's acts or thoughts in complete isolation has no social significance, and there is no way of measuring it.

The paramount influence of social situations is well illustrated by the experience of colonial administrators. Individual Africans, for example, who have attained to a high standard of technical proficiency when trained as agriculturists in a modern environment have, on returning to their own tribal community, ' forgotten ' or abstained from applying what they have learnt. They break off contact with the market economy because they are afraid of being isolated from or incurring the ill-will of their fellows should they practise modern methods. They are happier to use again the methods of their forefathers, and to be at one with the objectives of the community in which they again desire to live.

What is the significance of this type of behaviour? Is it not the renunciation by such people of the objectives and ideals which dominate, or are assumed to dominate, advanced societies? Is it not a renunciation of the accounting symbolism on which the European economy in the West is generally based?

This accounting symbolism expresses the system of value coefficients which, as Ragnar Frisch has shown,[1] must be

---

[1] As an example of such a system of value coefficients he writes : ' We may take the market prices of the goods. We may specify the concept of market prices further by saying that it should be prices actually paid by the buyer. With this specification—and with certain supplementary conventions for such items as the product of housewives' work or other products of the household—it will in most actual cases be clearly defined what sums should go into the basic magnitudes. This definition becomes a meaningful one because in order to define the value concept used, we have had recourse to some criterion outside the ecocirc-system itself. We have established the definition by referring to the concrete facts surrounding each individual payment. We may, if

established by ' some sort of convention ' which in itself is an axiomatic datum without which the sectional—or national—accounting streams with which we may be concerned have no meaning. As he rightly stresses, all the definitional equations of the ecocirc-system hold good ' whatever the system of value coefficients used, *provided only that the same system is applied throughout* ' (my italics). Our problem, however, arises precisely because we are dealing with different value systems and conventions. And thus the concept of abstract welfare has been and is being used as a bridge—but in my opinion an inadequate bridge—between different incomparable welfare systems.

Mr. Colin Clark, in criticizing the view of some modern theoretical economists that it is impossible to compare the level of income between two communities,[1] argues that exponents of this view ' do not realise what an intellectual anarchy they will let loose if their theories are adopted '. ' Deprive economics of the concept of welfare,' he writes, ' and what have you left ? Nothing : except possibly the theory of the trade cycle, where all values may be capable of expression in money terms without the introduction of the concept of welfare '. He does not hesitate to make ' comparisons of economic welfare of different times, places, and groups of people,' and writes :

' To compare for instance the real value of $0.795 produced per hour worked in U.S.A. in 1929, and 1.28 Rm., or $0.305 at par of exchange, produced per hour worked in Germany in the same year, we must take account of the actual quantities of goods and services produced, or, in other words, what the money will buy. The average American over that period spent his income in a certain way, purchasing certain quantities of goods and services. If he had gone to Germany and had set out to purchase exactly the same goods and services, he would have found that they were 0.9 per cent cheaper in the aggregate than in his own country. The German with his income purchased certain goods and services, by no means in the same proportion as the American. He spent much less of his income on motor cars and rent, and much more on food. The German going to America and purchasing the goods and services

we wish, establish the value definition by some other sort of convention, for instance, by an elaborate system of social valuations or socially determined priority figures, etc., but in all cases we must postulate some system of value coefficients before the basic concepts get a meaning.' 'Attempt at Clarification of Certain National Income Concepts '. cf. Stencil Memo 8th October, 1949. University Institute of Economics, Oslo.
[1] Cf. Colin Clark : *The Conditions of Economic Progress*, 2nd Edition, pp. 16–17.

which he was accustomed to consume would find that they were 19.8 per cent dearer. In comparing the real value of incomes in the two countries we must therefore allow something between 19.8 and 0.9 per cent for the difference in net purchasing power of money.'

He then discusses Fisher's and Pigou's well-known formulae for doing this.

This example, I suggest, exposes the hidden assumption on which Colin Clark is working : that either an American in Germany or a German in America could spend his income *as if* the fact that he was from a different society would not affect the purposes for which he desires or spends income. It may, of course, be argued that the social objectives of Germans and Americans are, on the whole, similar ; that a German can adapt himself relatively easily to the American way of life when he goes to America, and vice versa. But when comparing developed and under-developed, or industrial and pre-industrial, societies this argument is quite unreal. An American prepared to live in China as the Chinese do might be able to obtain specific goods and services more cheaply than these could be obtained in America. But if he wishes to live there as an American the position might be quite different. And the real question—which Colin Clark does not face—is : Are we comparing ' income ' in terms of the American or the Chinese *way of life* when we make such calculations ? For, obviously, the experience of isolated, ' atomized ' individuals living in foreign communities is of no comparative interest whatsoever.

Professor Kuznets no doubt had this point in mind when he quoted Colin Clark's figures showing that more than half the population of pre-industrial countries receive a per capita income of less than $40 in international units, and asked : ' Could people live in the United States during 1925–34 for several years on an income substantially below $40 per capita'? ' The answer', he thought, ' would be " yes ", if they were sufficiently wealthy to have lots of possessions to sell, sufficiently lucky to have rich relations or sufficiently bold to rob other people. The one-third to one-half of the pre-industrial population of the world would scarcely be in that position ; and if we assume that all they have produced and could consume per capita was less than 40 international units for several

D

years, the conclusion would be all would be dead by now.'
He is led to infer, therefore, ' (*a*) either that the estimates,
even after the customary adjustments for comparability with
industrial countries, are still deficient in omitting many goods
produced in pre-industrial countries ; or (*b*) in fact the whole
complex of goods produced and consumed is so different that
we cannot establish any equivalence of the type represented
by Mr. Clark's international units.'[1]

II. THE SYMBOLISM OF ECONOMIC ACTIVITY

These difficulties of comparison, I believe, are in no small
measure due to the concept of income which governs what
might be called the symbolism of economic activity in
economic literature (though not necessarily always in the
minds of the economic actors themselves), in the advanced
and complex money economies of the modern world.

That symbolism consists in the belief, as I show later
in this essay, that the members of such societies are engaged
in creating, and strive to increase, and, indeed, to maximize,
certain individual, abstract, psychological entities called
utilities, or satisfactions which reside in, or take the form of
individual states of consciousness. At this point I wish merely
to stress that even if this mental symbolism were found to be
an accurate portrayal of reality in ' advanced ' societies I would
argue that it had little or no parallel in the social and economic
life of most of the inhabitants of the ' under-developed '
countries of the world. In the economically ' backward '

---

[1] Professor Kuznets adds : ' The form in which the question was raised—how it is
possible for a large proportion of the population in pre-industrial countries to survive
on an income that produced, for several years, less than the equivalent of $40 per year
—obviously reflects my bias as a member of an industrial society. Personal experience
and observation tell me that such an annual product is well below the starvation level.
But were I a member of a pre-industrial society I might well have asked how it is possible
for the majority of the population in the United States to dispose of as much as $500
per year, or whatever its equivalent would be in international units of rupees or yuan.
Especially, on being told that of this huge income less than 10 per cent is saved for net
additions to capital stock, I might well ask how the population manages to consume so
much—given the limited amount of food one can eat, clothes one can wear, or houses
one can inhabit. And a suspicion similar to that voiced above could be entertained,
namely, that these income figures for industrial countries must include many categories
of items that are *not* included in income as ordinarily conceived in pre-industrial countries ; and that the whole pattern of consumption and living in industrial countries is
so different as to explain the ease with which these *huge quantities* of goods are produced
and especially consumed.'

communities economic activity cannot possibly be regarded as governed by highly refined individual choices or abstract evaluations directed towards increasing individual mental satisfactions. For the most part these peoples are engaged in narrow economic pursuits circumscribed by an environment from which they have, as yet, learned to wring only a precarious existence in accordance with the traditional social and economic precepts to which they still cling. To speak in their case of the creation of income in a monetary, a psychological, or even an individual sense is to apply a foreign symbolism to express, or to account for, activities which are not conducted in terms of such symbolism, and cannot be expressed by it.

By far the greater part of the activities of such societies are directed to the production of goods and services to satisfy the ' concrete ' needs of immediate or seasonal consumption and not in any sense to the creation of 'rights' to goods and services or ' values ' in the abstract—such as the right to an abstract stream of ' income ' in an accounting or proprietary sense. That is why we meet so frequently, in such communities, with the well-known phenomenon that when particular goods or services are traded against money, production is not necessarily stimulated by higher prices for them, or by higher rewards to labour. On the contrary higher prices may result in a falling off both of production and of the supply of labour : what stimulates the people concerned is the achievement of particular limited purposes —purposes which are socially determined by custom and tradition. In such societies money is only one ' good ' among other goods, and it has limited uses. What money is, and what role is assigned to it, is always an expression of the institutional arrangements of society as a whole—a truth often forgotten even in ' advanced ' societies. The individual accumulation of money, as for example, in societies where the possession of it can do little to affect the willingness, or ability, of persons to alter traditional patterns of economic activity (e.g. when it cannot be used to acquire land, or property-rights or other resources, or to employ labour for other than traditionally determined purposes) is of little use to the individual. It does not necessarily even yield him increased security since this also may be determined by social forces which the possession of money cannot necessarily control.

The main point which, I suggest, emerges from an examination of economic activity in most under-developed societies is that it cannot be expressed adequately by highly abstract concepts of individual income in accounting or monetary terms ; to attempt to do so is to do violence to their traditional systems of social organization and evaluation : just as one would do violence to the values created in the family if one were to try to express them only in terms of the ' income ' yielded to each of its members ; or to regard its mutual co-operant activity as based only on the desire to magnify their individual satisfactions.

It is not only the fact that a very limited range of the activities of pre-industrial societies may be covered by accounting symbolisms of any kind that makes comparison with more advanced societies difficult. There is the further important consideration that the pre-industrial societies are, in most cases, undergoing rapid transition. They are in a process of disintegration ; rapid changes are occurring in their way of life and in their social value systems ; members of the society are becoming attached to modern money economies in which value systems are entirely different. How can one compare the income of ' individuals ' or ' groups ' at different times when they have been subject to such changes? How can one attempt to assess whether the pre-industrial community is ' better off ' when, as in South Africa, for example, it has undergone a rapid process of urbanization, and has been integrated into a modern economy in a quite different social framework?

The income which we record for such groups in their new modern environment portray only the new objectively recorded relations between them and others. But the accounting records tell us nothing of interest concerning the value of the social system which has been destroyed as compared with the one which has taken its place.

III. AN UNRESOLVED DICHOTOMY

At the root of all these difficulties of definition and comparability there lies, I believe, an unresolved dichotomy in the meaning ascribed to national income aggregates. This is due to the fact that, although the process of measuring the national income is a strictly accounting procedure, the aggregates so obtained are frequently used for purposes which transcend the accounting relations which can alone be expressed by them. It is precisely this extension of the concept of income which belongs to one category of logical thought, to express something such as welfare or ' ecfare '[1] which falls into another category of thought, and cannot be expressed in accounting terms at all, which is responsible for the state of disillusionment with ' welfare economics '.

This dichotomy cannot be avoided by a flight into neutral concepts designed to by-pass the problem, for example by measuring changes in productivity in order to avoid ' value ' judgments. Indeed not even the use of such specially manufactured words as ' ecfare ' will help us out of the difficulty. This is so not only because the mere calculation of statistical aggregates divorced from social reality and purpose is valueless, and indeed dangerous in that it results in the creation of an empty symbolism in place of realistic goals of social action, but because it avoids the fundamental issue— namely, whether the logical principles which lie at the root of the procedure are valid.

It will be the main thesis of this essay that it is a logical fallacy to regard the satisfaction or utility which (it is alleged) is ' yielded ' by, or derived from, goods and services as ' income ' in any meaningful sense, because the term ' income ' is an accounting term and can only meaningfully express an accounting relation. I submit that the assumption that there are comparable abstract private criteria or values embedded in an individual's stream of consciousness which represent income as something other than, additional to, or a counter-part of purely accounting relations recorded in objective transactions—' income ' which is thought to be the ' stuff ' out of which welfare is constructed—is a fiction ; and I submit that the belief that the simple comparision of account-ing aggregates between different societies indicates something

[1] To use a term which Professor Robertson substitutes ' partly for brevity and partly in the hope of craftily dispelling the notion that the phrase ' economic welfare ' is bulging with ethics and emotiveness ', in ' Utility and All That ' (*Manchester School Studies*, May 1951, p. 130).

more than the specific accounting relations which such aggregates alone portray is untenable.

In order to develop this thesis I must crave the reader's indulgence for an unavoidable detour along well-worn paths as it is necessary to re-examine some of the basic definitions and analytical procedures of the two pioneers in this field, Pigou and Irving Fisher.

IV. LOGICAL LIMITATIONS TO INCOME COMPARISONS

Pigou,[1] in defining economic welfare as ' that *part* of social welfare that can be brought directly or indirectly into relation with the measuring rod of money ', was not primarily concerned with measuring ' economic welfare '[2] in order to obtain a barometer or index of total welfare, nor to discover how large total welfare is, but how its magnitude *would be affected* ' by the introduction of causes which it is in the power of statesmen or private persons to call into being '. Indeed, he emphasizes this view by saying that ' though the whole may consist of many varying parts, so that a change in one part never *measures* the change in the whole, yet the change in the part may always *affect* the change in the whole by its full amount '. Thus

' it will not, indeed, tell us how total welfare *after the introduction of an economic cause*, will differ from what it was before, but it will tell us how total welfare will differ from what it would have been if that cause had not been introduced '.

Moreover, he specifically states :

' It will be sufficient to lay down more or less dogmatically two propositions ; first, that the elements of welfare are *states of consciousness* and, perhaps, their relations ; secondly, that welfare can be brought under the category of greater or less.' (My italics.)[3]

---

[1] All quotations from Pigou are from *The Economics of Welfare* unless otherwise indicated.

[2] To Pigou the two concepts, economic welfare and the national dividend, are co-ordinate, and ' just as economic welfare is that *part* of total welfare which can be brought directly or indirectly into relation with a money measure, so the national dividend is that part of the objective income of the community . . . which can be measured in money '.

[3] In a note on ' Real Income and Economic Welfare ' (*Oxford Economic Papers*, February 1951) Professor Pigou now concludes that it is only in one case out of the three which he discusses that ' inferences about economic welfare are possible ', and that in others ' no inferences about changes in economic welfare can be drawn from price quantity statistics '. I am not, however, concerned in this paper with the practical difficulties of interpreting price quantity statistics. My analysis is designed to show that *welfare inferences from them (irrespective of the number of cases) are either logically invalid or necessarily tautologous as when economic welfare has already been defined in terms of the very goods and services which can be measured by price quantity statistics.*

Indeed in his most recent article he writes :

'What do we mean by the economic welfare of an individual? It will be generally agreed that this must be somehow resident in his state of mind or consciousness. When we speak loosely of 'material welfare', in the sense of a man's income or possessions, that is not welfare, as we are thinking of it here. Material welfare may be a *means* to welfare, but it certainly is not identical with or *a part of it*. As it seems to me, welfare must be taken to refer either to the goodness of a man's state of mind or to the satisfactions embodied in it.' (Italics in the original.)[1]

Now I suggest that the goods and services which we are, or believe ourselves capable of, bringing, directly or indirectly, into relationship with the measuring-rod of money are not one set of data or events, while the welfare which Pigou regards as following from them, directly or indirectly, is another set of data or events. To say that a man has more of certain goods and services and that his welfare will consequently be increased because he has them is to speak of two series of events where there is only one. In accordance with this definition of welfare, i.e. *as expressed in terms of goods and services*, welfare will necessarily be increased or diminished as the amount of goods and services is increased or diminished. *As defined*, they are a part of some larger whole which we can describe as his welfare as a whole—but logically speaking an increase or decrease in the amount of goods and services does not affect his total welfare, except only by the increase or decrease in the amount of those goods and services themselves, i.e. in so far as welfare has been defined in terms of goods and services.

The national dividend represents an arbitrary addition of certain gross or net values arbitrarily ascribed by society, or by the *national income calculator*, to certain events or happenings perceived by human beings. They are usually those events which take the form of goods and services which can more or less readily be so valued or measured. But in adding up such a series of events or happenings and calling the total the national dividend, we must not imagine that they throw light on yet another series of events or happenings.

It is this manner of looking at the national dividend as a

[1] 'Some Aspects of Welfare Economics', *American Economic Review*, June 1951, p. 288.

counterpart of something else which, I believe, is responsible for the dichotomy to which I have referred. It is one of those types of mistake, which as Professor Ryle has explained,[1] arises from representing facts ' as if they belonged to one logical type or category . . . when they actually belong to another '. Among other illustrations he gives the following :

'A foreigner visiting Oxford or Cambridge for the first time is shown a number of colleges, libraries, playing fields, museums, scientific departments and administrative offices. He then asks " But where is the University? I have seen where the members of the Colleges live, where the Registrar works, where the scientists experiment and the rest. But I have not yet seen the University in which reside and work the members of your University ". It has then to be explained to him that the University is not another collateral institution, some ulterior counterpart to the colleges, laboratories, and offices which he has seen. The University is just the way in which all that he has already seen is organized. When they are seen and when their co-ordination is understood, the University has been seen. His mistake lay in his innocent assumption that it was correct to speak of Christ Church, the Bodleian Library, the Ashmolean Museum, *and* the University, to speak, that is as if " the University " stood for an extra member of the class of which these other units are members. He was mistakenly allocating the University to the same category as that to which the other institutions belong.'

Now I suggest that when, by using a common unit of account, we add up ' net values ' of certain events or happenings (goods and services) we are simply ' *measuring* ' certain *parts* of a larger whole, just as if we were describing different parts of the University. It would be as wrong to regard these goods and services as *causing* welfare as it would be to regard the different buildings as *causing* the University. The University is not a *counterpart* to its teachers and buildings ; nor is society's welfare a *counterpart* of its goods and services. Similarly, when we say that we have measured the increase in the value of goods and services produced in a society, we cannot then proceed to speak about this increase causing a further increase in the welfare (or ' ecfare ') of society. An increase in the amount of goods and services does not affect the total welfare of society, except *by definition* through this very increase or decrease in such goods and services themselves.

[1] Gilbert Ryle : *The Concept of Mind*, Hutchinsons University Library, 1949, p. 16. I am greatly indebted for permission to quote from this book and to Professor Ryle personally for valuable suggestions.

Pigou is thinking of the national dividend as an objective counterpart of something else, i.e. of subjective experiences. But it is, I submit, logically fallacious to imply that because we can ' measure ' some of the former we can thereby imply or measure the latter.

What I should like to stress particularly at this point is, however, that it is not a change in the national dividend or measurable net money income, as narrowly defined, which *causes* a change in welfare, but that it is a change in what is, by habit, custom, or belief, regarded by the society as constituting welfare which determines the nature, and frequently the amount, of the national dividend itself. In terms of Professor Ryle's analogy, it is the idea of what the University is or should be which determines how its constituent parts will grow or be permitted to grow, and not vice versa. It is the ultimate (conscious or unconscious) purpose for which those events we call ' income ' are desired that determines the nature and extent of the forms in which income will be incorporated. We cannot, therefore, compare ' income ' aggregates for different societies, or even ' evaluate ' income in them, without taking into account the social purposes and system which govern the creation of income. A society which glorifies war will have a different ' system or concept of welfare ' and hence different concepts of what is ' income ' from one which desires peace. It is said of the Bushmen of South Africa that no attempts to bring them to adopt the social life of a modern community were at any time successful. They remained hunters—notwithstanding their high intelligence, capability of practising arable agriculture and of creating other goods and services—because they liked hunting. Hunting was their ideal form of welfare ; and, therefore, ' income ' to the Bushmen (if we can use the word in this context at all) was defined in terms of success in the chase and in the sustenance yielded by the chase alone. Such ' income ' could not be compared with ' equivalent ' goods and services which might have resulted from some other form of activity, or with ' income ' in a society of non-hunters.

The income-creating process is itself part and parcel of the income it yields, and the results of the process cannot be abstracted from the process itself. It is inadmissible to ' evaluate ' the activity of hunting merely by the number of animals caught, and still more fallacious to compare the figure so obtained with, say, the ' value ' of meat obtained by another society from the slaughter of domestic beasts. The activity and the income are inseparable and are both embedded together in the customs and ways of thought which mould the social life of the community as a whole.

In other words, the relation between total welfare and economic welfare or income (Pigou's national income or dividend) is a relationship similar to that between the rules, laws, constitutional arrangements, habits, institutional patterns, and beliefs which govern society and the results of the social activities so regulated. It is a relationship similar to that between the rules according to which a game is played, the playing of the game, and the points in which the score is reckoned. To identify, or seek for, a functional relationship between income and total welfare is as logically fallacious as to identify the points scored in playing a game with the ' value ' of the game to the players.

As I endeavour to show below, when we speak of, for example, ' the maximization of income ' we are using a term with strictly limited meaning—one which is meaningful only as an accounting expression, the expression being implicitly subsumed under the accounting ' laws ' or rules which we have adopted for that kind of reckoning. It would be absurd to speak of maximizing the rules of the game itself. The game of chess is played in accordance with certain prescribed and generally accepted rules. If we so desire we can measure, evaluate, or account the skill of the player according to an accepted scale of points or awards and penalties. The player, by the exercise of appropriate skill, could thus maximize his points or ' earnings '. But we cannot meaningfully assess the ' welfare ' or psychic income, or utility or pleasure flowing from the game of chess to the player by adding up the score.

It is logically as fallacious to speak of maximizing total welfare as it is to speak of maximizing the University. The total welfare of society is not some ' ulterior counterpart ' to the production of goods and services which can be measured in money ; nor does it consist only of those events which cannot be so measured ; nor is it necessary for an understanding of it to postulate states of consciousness, ' psychic income, and the like.

When we examine the different activities of society, both those which can and those which cannot be expressed or symbolized in accounting terms as income, we are examining aspects of its welfare. Society's total welfare is just the way in which all these activities are organized. When they are perceived and assessed, and when their system of ordering and co-ordination has been described and grasped, the total welfare of society has been, *ipso facto*, assessed also. To speak as if total welfare stood for an extra member of the class of which these other activities are members is mistakenly to allocate total welfare to the same category as that to which the other institutions which govern the activities of society belong.

I submit that this analysis shows how dangerous it is to embark too hastily on international and indeed inter-temporal comparisons between income aggregates.

To endeavour to assess and compare ' welfare ' merely by comparing national income aggregates for societies with different laws, rules, conventions, hopes, and ideals is as fallacious as to try to assess the pleasure which a pair of players derive from playing dominoes, and then compare it with that yielded to another pair engaged in playing chess, by comparing the points scored by the players in each game.

Where the system of rules, the social order of preference, or the value system as a whole is different, comparisons of parts of each system are invalid unless those parts are related to some external objective standard of measurement. Thus it is meaningful to compare the average expectation of life in different communities, or the incidence of different diseases, or the number of calories of food, *if we are agreed as to the purpose for which we make such comparisons* ; but if our laws, rules, or conventions differ as to the importance of any of these, comparison itself can tell us very little.

I submit that the belief that we can readily compare national income aggregates between greatly differing societies is, in the last resort, to be explained by a peculiar assumption which underlies the concept of income in ' advanced ' Western societies, namely, that the individual possesses certain essentially private criteria (or even that welfare *consists in having* certain private units of something) according to which he alone can assess his welfare ; criteria which are inaccessible to, and which cannot be objectively assessed by, others ; criteria which are to be found in individual states of consciousness and can therefore only be measured indirectly.

On this assumption it is argued that, if we can measure in money terms the goods and services which make up the ' income ' of these individuals, we can infer and assess the *private* values or criteria, the inner stream of consciousness, the satisfaction or the utility, which individuals, *irrespective of the society to which they belong*, enjoy. It is implied, then, that international comparisons of income are meaningful precisely because such comparisons refer to this abstract entity—this individual ' income ' ; ' income ', namely, which is dissociated from the specific social context in which it is embedded, and which all individuals ' enjoy ' irrespective of the society to which they belong.

V.   ' PSYCHIC ' AND 'ACCOUNTING ' INCOME

What is ' welfare ' or ' economic welfare ' to Pigou was ' psychic or enjoyment income ' to Irving Fisher. This psychic theory of income is by no means of merely historical interest. In my opinion it is, notwithstanding many modern devices to escape from it, still embedded in our ways of thought.[1]

To Fisher ' income ' is a series of events,[2] but the events he regards as constituting ' ultimate income ' for each individual ' are *only* those events which come within the purview of his individual experience '. It is the abstract ' psychic experience of the individual mind ' with which Fisher is concerned. To him ultimate income is nothing if not a *private process of observing* (and privately measuring) these *inner* events of enjoyment : the counterpart of real income— a counterpart located in the ' mind ' of the observer. It is as if, while eating my dinner, I am observing, recording, or reporting to myself on the ' agreeable sensation ' and experi-

---

[1] See, for example, the quotation from Kenneth E. Boulding below, and my subsequent remarks.

[2] *The Theory of Interest*, pp. 1 and 5.

ence of eating it ; and it is as if I calculate or measure my *net* psychic income by not only continually observing, recording, and reporting on ' agreeable sensations '—if that is possible —but also by observing and reporting on accompanying disagreeable ones (such as those which Fisher calls the ' labour pains ' involved in earning income) and deducting the latter from the former.

Herein also lies the source of the belief that somehow the goods and services which an individual receives are the *cause* of welfare—the cause, namely, of something additional to them : something which occurs in the minds of individuals.

I submit that this concept of the relation between measurable ' income ' and welfare is simply a para-mechanical hypothesis, the dangers of which Professor Ryle has so trenchantly exposed. It is based on that type of category mistake which he has called ' the category mistake which underlies the dogma of the ghost in the machine '. He states that, in unconscious reliance upon this dogma,[1]

' Theorists and laymen alike constantly construe the adjectives by which we characterise performances as ingenious, wise, methodical, careful, witty, etc., as signalising the occurrence in someone's hidden stream of consciousness of special processes functioning as ghostly harbingers or more specifically as occult causes of the performances so characterised.'

But in opposition to this entire dogma he argues that :

' in describing the workings of a person's mind we are not describing a second set of shadowy operations. We are describing certain phases of his one career ; namely, we are describing the ways in which parts of his conduct are managed. . . . When a person talks sense aloud, ties knots, feints or sculpts . . . he for a person is bodily active and he is mentally active, but he is not being synchronously active in two different " places".'

I submit that in defining ultimate income as enjoyment or psychic income, and as the ' inner events of the mind ' Fisher[2] falls into the type of category mistake which we have been discussing. This psychic income is not an event or happening which ' occurs ' somewhere, i.e. in a person's mind, and is ' caused ' by another ' external ' event or happening, for example, by the receipt of goods and services by that person. To ask where and when does the psychic income occur would

---

[1] Op. cit., p. 50.   [2] Op. cit., p. 4.

be like asking, for example, concerning the meaning of an expression, ' when and where do these meanings occur? ' . . . 'The phrase "what such and such an expression means" does not describe a thing or happening at all, and *a fortiori* not an occult thing or happening'.[1] Eating my dinner and enjoying it are not two events but one. 'We do . . . things because we like doing them, or want to do them, and not because we like or want something accessory to them. . . . The angler would not accept or understand an offer of the pleasures without the activities of angling. It is angling that he enjoys, not something that angling engenders '.[2]

The agreeable sensations which Fisher would have us believe are the stuff of which ultimate psychic income is made are not things or episodes. It is therefore ' nonsense to speak of observing, inspecting, witnessing, or scrutinizing them ' ; and it is, I submit, equally nonsense to try, as Fisher would have us try, to ' measure ' them, however indirectly, ' since the objects proper to such verbs are things and episodes '.

It does not make sense to speak of my observing, scrutinizing, reporting on, being conscious of, inferring, or *measuring* that I am enjoying the eating of my dinner. If it did, then ' it would seem to make sense to ask whether, according to the doctrine, I am not also conscious of being conscious of inferring,[3] that is, in a position to say " Here I am, spotting the fact that here I am deducing such and such from so and so ". And then there would be no stopping place ; there would have to be an infinite number of onion-skins of consciousness embedding any mental state or process whatsoever.'

Now it is precisely this infinite regression in the thing we are trying to ' measure ' which puzzled Fisher and which, I submit, underlies the dichotomy to which I have referred. What we call the 'measurement' or 'calculation' of the national income is nothing more or less than the application of accounting principles to certain types of economic data. Fisher was an early pioneer in this field. To him accounting was 'not a mere makeshift, but a complete, consistent, and logical system'. In critically applying it he aimed, firstly, at making the most

[1] Gilbert Ryle, op. cit., p. 295.
[2] Gilbert Ryle, op. cit., p. 132.
[3] Gilbert Ryle, op. cit., p. 163.

igid logical distinction between the nature of capital and
ncome. He wished to avoid the heterogeneous combination
of ' commodities ' and ' services ' ; the first he regarded as
concrete wealth and the other as the abstract use of it.[1] His
second main objective was to elucidate that what we call the
measurement of income is but the drawing up of a system of
accounts. The significant feature of any consistent system
of accounts is always that in it every receipt of ' income '
appearing on the debit side of the account is exactly offset
by an equal item of ' outgo ' on the credit side. Thus the
process of book-keeping ' amounts to a continued series of
snapshots of the train of enterprise moving through time '.[2]
Even a profit and loss account covering a period between the
dates of two balance-sheets is only a detailed reconstruction
of how the capital accounts changed as between the two
dates of the balance-sheets.

Unfortunately, however, under double-entry book-keeping
transactions only can be recorded, and a transaction involves
the passing of money or money's worth. This fact immediately brings us up against Fisher's central difficulty, namely,
that ' money receipts ', as he says,[3] may be ' good makeshifts
for *true* income [my italics], but even from a practical point of
view they will not always serve, while as a matter of strict
theory they are always wrong. They could be right only
under the condition that *all* income, *from whatever source* [my
italics], flowed through the cash drawer.' If it were true that
' the flow out of that drawer consisted exclusively of expenditures for each and every satisfaction as it occurred, then the
flow of money through the cash drawer would serve as a

---

[1] 'To bring about homogeneity', he writes, 'we could exclude *uses* altogether and
confine " income " to concrete commodities'; or '*we could exclude commodities
altogether and restrict the term to uses*'. (My italics.) ' The only true method,' he
insists, ' is to regard uniformly as income the *service* of a dwelling to its owner (shelter
or money rental), the *service* of a piano (music), and the service of food (nourishment) ;
and in the same uniform manner to exclude alike from the category of income the
dwelling, the piano, and even the food. These are capital, not income ; . . . *Their income
follows later in the form of piano music and nourishment.*' (My italics.) *The Nature of Capital
and Income*, pp. 105–6 (New York and London, 1919).
  It is this extension of the use of the accounting term ' income ' to cover *the process
of consumption* which I analyse and criticize in the text above. Fisher's distinction
between capital and income in an accounting sense is, however, extremely important
and is still frequently overlooked.
[2] W. J. Busschau, *Measure of Gold*, p. 17 (South Africa, 1949).
[3] Cf. *The Nature of Capital and Income*, p. 137.

true measure of income, and the cash drawer might be called a sort of income *meter*'. But, in fact, ' not all income passes through the meter. Some passes around it, as, for instance, the shelter derived from a man's own house or the comforts from his own furniture . . . .'[1]

Here we come to the crux of the matter, for in order to overcome the inherent logical distinction between what can and what cannot be expressed in accounting terms—between what takes place in the transactions of the market-place and is recorded in money terms (or its equivalent) and what is never so recorded, i.e. the utility or satisfaction yielded by commodities when finally consumed (which Fisher calls the abstract use of wealth *and which he regards as ' true ' income*)—Fisher has to invent a bridge between two logically different and incompatible categories of thought. He has to go beyond the system of accounts of the market-place; for in the case of real persons, i.e. final consumers, the two sides of the account containing only such *recorded* transactions do not finally balance, because the accounts do not, as to be consistent they should, consist solely of double entries. On the contrary, the income and outgo accounts of such ' real persons ' contain a residue of items which will not pair, e.g., the shelter of a person's home, use of furniture, use of food, use of clothes, etc. For, of course, those items constitute a kind of ' income ' (i.e. the final ' use ' of those commodities) which does not appear elsewhere as ' outgo '. There always remains, when applying the accounting system to real persons, ' some *outer fringe* (my italics) of uncancelled income.'[2] All other services are merely preparatory to such services, and pass themselves on from one category of capital to another. Thus the ' income ' from investments, being deposited in a bank, is ' outgo ' with respect to the bank account; the bank account yields

---

[1] It should again be noted that, to Fisher, ' The income from any instrument is therefore the flow of abstract services rendered by that instrument '—unlike capital which is a fund at an instant of time and consists of concrete wealth. The word ' flow ', however, is apt to be very misleading in any case, because in fact in dealing with transactions we do not measure a flow at all in the sense of measuring, say, the flow of water past a certain point over a period of time. What we do is to construct a balance-sheet at different points of time, and the construction of balance-sheets involves evaluation of assets at these different points of time. But evaluation of assets in that sense involves the introduction of an ideal or standard income.

[2] Which consists of what economists have usually called consumption (Fisher, *The Nature of Capital and Income*, p. 164).

' income ' by paying for stocks and bonds, food, etc., but in each case the same item enters as ' outgo ' with respect to these and other categories of capital. In all these cases the individual receives no ' income ' which is not at the same time ' outgo '. It is only as he consumes the food, wears the clothes, or uses the furniture that he receives ' income '.

What is significant in Fisher's approach is that to overcome this dichotomy he invents a fiction similar to the one which is usually employed to obtain the symmetry of a double-entry accounting system in connexion with the investment made by the proprietors of a business in that business. This fiction consists in our conventionally regarding such a business or venture as something *apart or dissociated* from its proprietors. So Fisher employs, as a last resort, the fiction that the body as a transforming instrument is something *apart or dissociated* from its ' proprietor ', namely, ' the mind ' to which the ' body ' pays out final (or ' true ') income, which final income, he argues, is not received until, as subjective income, it emerges into ' the stream of consciousness of any human being '[1]—a concept which, as I have shown, is on all fours with that held by Pigou concerning the ultimate nature of ' welfare '.

Many examples in Fisher's book show how powerfully he was influenced by this attempt to complete the system of accounts of the workaday world by extending it to the realms of the mind ; for example

'. . . if we include the body as a transforming instrument, while we must *credit* with their respective services all these outside agencies, such as, food, clothing, dwelling, furniture, ornaments and other articles which, as it were, bombard a man's sensory system, we must also at the same time *debit* the body with the same items. In this case the only surviving credit items after these equal debits and credits are cancelled are the resulting final satisfactions in the human mind.'[2] (My italics.)

Now it will be immediately apparent that, if we accept this concept of ' ultimate ' or ' true ' income based on fictional mental accounting, we would have to postulate another ' mind ' or skin of consciousness in which the mental accounting is conducted. But then, as Professor Ryle has demonstrated, ' there would be no stopping place in an infinite number of such minds or states of consciousness '.

[1] *The Nature of Capital and Income*. p. 168.   [2] Ibid., p. 167.

E

For clearly the net psychic income (negative or positive) could only be calculated by 'balancing off' the mental accounts at different time-intervals. If, for example, exertion, labour, pain, anxiety, or trouble is expended by a person in obtaining durable goods in period 1, but these only begin to be consumed in period 2, does the person keep a mental 'income' and 'outgo' or a mental 'profit and loss' account? Does he carry in his mind a mental capital account? When he receives a new suit of clothes does he make a mental debit entry, e.g. 'To Unconsumed Satisfaction', and a mental credit entry to that account whenever he wears the suit? When a person has paid for his education or physical training does he keep a mental capital account showing this investment, and does he credit himself with the 'income' it yields to him in the future? If he does indeed conduct these peculiar operations in his mind it would be most interesting to know when they occur—hourly, daily, weekly, or annually!

VI. LIMITS TO MEASUREMENT

I have dealt at length with Fisher's abortive attempt to build an artificial bridge between an accounting and a psychic concept of income, in order to show that such concepts as 'income', 'outgo', 'receipts', and 'expenditure' can only be meaningfully used as accounting concepts and cannot be extended to embrace 'income' in a psychological sense. Until we realize this clearly we cannot hope to rid ourselves of serious current confusions.

Even so constructive a thinker as Kenneth Boulding uses the words 'income' and 'outgo' in both an accounting and a psychological sense.[1] The distinction he makes between the pair of terms 'income' and 'outgo' on the one hand, and the pair of terms 'receipts' and 'expenditure' on the other hand, while interesting, does not get him out of this tangle since these are all accounting terms and can only refer to *recorded transactions*, until we come to Fisher's 'residue of items which will not pair', i.e. the 'consumption' of objective goods and services which cannot be expressed in accounting terms, unless we follow Fisher's attempt and postulate that the

[1] K. Boulding: *A Reconstruction of Economics*, 1950, pp. 139–41.

individual keeps subjective mental accounts with himself. And indeed Boulding ends up just as Fisher did by saying :

'When psychic capital is taken into consideration, however, it may be doubted whether there are any really non-durable goods. Even the things usually labelled as services, such as movies, in fact produce psychic capital with a limited rate of depreciation. We go to the movies in order to *produce the mental state* of just having gone to the movies. *This mental state is the commodity* which we purchase with the price of admission : it is a commodity which depreciates like every other commodity. For some individuals it depreciates rapidly, so that it has to be replaced in a week or less : in other individuals the rate of depreciation is slower, so that they do not have to go to another movie for a month or even several months.' (My italics.)

Moreover, to say, as Boulding does, that ' a farmer earns income as the value of his crop grows ' is to confuse capital and income on the one hand, and to fail to distinguish between ' standard ' and ' realized ' income on the other.[1] The growing crop does not represent the ' earnings ' of 'income'. Such growth can be ' reflected ' in a capital account which attempts to assess the value of income *in prospect*, but what *may eventually* be realized as income is not income that has been realized. Realized income is precisely that income which has been detached from capital by being converted into money (or into another recorded asset form) in a recorded transaction. It is the recorded *transaction* which shapes it as income in an *accounting* sense. Our measurement of ' income ' can logically refer only to income which has so been ' realized '. For only this income can enter into any form of accounting—which is basically a process of objective social evaluation. That such objective social evaluation, depending on ' market trans-actions', is never free from subjective hopes and expectations concerning the future, and that over large sectors of the economy transactions may be recorded which are not based on ' market ' valuations at all, does not alter the fact that there is a basic logical distinction between such *objective* evaluation and that procedure which I contend is illegitimate, namely, the use of accounting concepts to evaluate subjective processes which allegedly take place within a person's mind or within himself.

---

[1] Fisher rightly insisted on the fundamental logical distinction between the ideal (or standard) income and the actual (or realized) income.

The 'income' of which we can take account and 'measure' must, willy-nilly, refer only to *publicly disclosed* evaluations arising out of recorded transactions. If we wish to distinguish between 'consuming' and 'spending', the farthest point to which accounting can take us is to that objective balance-sheet which records the expenditure by a person on durable goods; but the use or consumption of these goods does not 'yield' income. To speak as if it does is to apply accounting concepts to a category of thought which it does not fit. One cannot speak of consumption yielding 'income' in the same sense as a bank account or stocks and shares yield 'income'. We do not, when we consume a piece of bread, speak of the bread yielding 'income', nor do we regard that portion of the bread which remains unconsumed as capital. To speak in this way would involve that process of mental accounting, the fallacious nature of which I have endeavoured to expose.

Private persons may of course keep private accounts which would indicate the change in the values of durable goods in their possession between two periods of time; but if one were to attempt to argue that persons keeping such accounts would thereby be measuring the 'income' they receive from the use of such goods (the fall in their value being taken to represent the income which has 'accrued' to the person in the intervening period), one would again be falling into a fallacious use of the word 'income', which really expresses an accounting *relation* and not something which is the counterpart of the using up of a durable good in the process of consumption.

Moreover, in this connexion one must avoid confusing windfall gains (or losses)—which might accrue to a person if he sold a durable good in the market—with income. Such gains (or losses) are not 'income' but capital appreciation (or depreciation) and are due to the society's valuation of expected future income; income, however, which is expected in the future is but the prospect of income—an ideal or target which may never be realized.

Now it is quite true that persons or fictitious persons can and do buy and sell prospects (and can thus individually realize in a true accounting sense windfall gains or losses made at the expense of other persons) which are changes on capital account ; but *for the whole system of social accounts* there can be no windfall gains or losses of this nature. Society as a whole cannot convert its prospects into income until time and good fortune have fulfilled them. Society cannot make a windfall gain or loss except in the sense in which a person can be said to gain where an *unexpected* pleasurable event occurs or lose when an *expected* pleasurable event fails to occur. If society tried to measure such psychological windfalls, it would be keeping a mental account with itself.[1] But no accounts can portray the relationship of a person to himself. Meaningful measurement ceases at the point at which persons acquire objective goods and services ; to go beyond is to enter the realm of hope and fancy.[2]

VII. Conclusion

It might appear that the previous analysis has led us to disconcerting conclusions, but I suggest that this is not the case. Once we cease to be misled by the mirage of fictional mental accounting, and by attempts to portray through very simple accounting aggregates the infinite variety in the value and preference systems of different societies with which we are confronted, we will free the welfare concept from a serious dichotomy of thought, and will realize that the mere calculation of accounting relations cannot in itself answer, and should not be expected to answer, questions the answers to which do not lie in the realm of measurement.

Moreover, we will realize that the accounts (and accounting symbolism) of different societies are not comparable ; that we cannot compare separate accounting aggregates for one society with those relating to another with a different social and economic framework, and hence a different system of accounting values. We cannot assume that what appears to

---

[1] Society can, however, like the individual, sell prospects (a capital transaction) to *other* societies. For example, the sale of mineral rights or prospects to foreigners (and the import of other goods in exchange). This illustration precisely indicates the difference between objective accounting transactions to which the terms capital and income can be applied and subjective ones to which they cannot.

[2] As Professor J. R. Hicks has so rightly concluded in his important book *Value and Capital* (p. 180) : '.. the concept of income ' ... is ' one which the positive theoretical economist only employs in his argument at his peril. For him income is a very dangerous term. ... '

be ' income ' in one society can be compared with ' income ' recorded in another, because since the ' income ' which we can grasp is an accounting relation and not a psychic entity what will be so recorded in the two different societies will differ in its significance according to the nature and ideals of the society itself.

Thus one of the main tasks which now confront economists, statisticians, and sociologists emerges more clearly, namely, to determine which factors constitute the welfare pattern—rather than to stop short at comparing symbols which do not adequately portray it. To say this, of course, raises many more questions than it answers. Perhaps I may be permitted to ask that supremely inconvenient question which has popped up its head throughout this article only to be resolutely suppressed : What do we gain by the complicated symbolism which pictures this mental thing—this alleged counterpart to reality—called Utility, Satisfaction, Welfare, Ecfare, or Plain Everyman's ' Equal Capacity to Enjoy Life ' which Scitovsky has now called it in discussing inter-personal comparisons of it ?[1] Thirty years after the publication of *The Economics of Welfare* Pigou is, like so many others, still of the opinion that ' if the satisfaction of different individuals cannot be compared, a large part of that subject (Welfare Economics) is undermined ', and he comforts himself with the conclusion that ' on the basis of analogy, observation and intercourse, interpersonal comparisons *can* properly be made ; and, moreover, unless we have a special reason to believe the contrary, a given amount of stuff may be presumed to yield a similar amount of satisfaction, not indeed as between *any* one man and any other, but as between representative members and groups of individuals, such as the citizens of Birmingham and the citizens of Leeds. This is all we need to allow this branch of Welfare Economics to function.' (Italics in the original.)

But why do we need this fictional comparison at all ? For the interpersonal comparison which Pigou here apparently succeeds in making rests not on the essential comparability of this abstract ' utility ' or ' satisfaction ' in the minds of different individuals. The comparison appears to succeed only because ' the given amount of stuff ' which according to

[1] ' The State of Welfare Economics,' *American Economic Review*, June 1951.

Pigou ' may be presumed to yield it (utility) ' is by implication comparable on the hidden assumption that the citizens of Birmingham and of Leeds have broadly similar tastes and thus demand broadly similar kinds of ' stuff ' ; just as Marshall took it for granted that ' it would naturally be assumed that a shilling's worth of gratification to one Englishman might be taken as equivalent with a shilling's worth to another. . . until cause to the contrary was shown.'[1] In other words, the ' welfare ' *yielded* by the ' stuff ' is assumed to be equal *because* the welfare pattern itself was first assumed to be the same. Thus the utility or satisfaction was found to be apparently comparable in the abstract, precisely and only because it had already been defined *ab initio* as flowing from, yielded by, and dependent on the same ' real ' things. That the inter-personal comparison of abstract utility rests on such circular reasoning becomes finally obvious if we take a different case and try to compare the satisfactions of the citizens of Birmingham not with those of Leeds but with the satisfactions yielded by a given amount of ' stuff ' peculiar to the customs, say, of an African tribe prone to cannibalism and the like. The abstract satisfactions would not be regarded as comparable—and why not ?—precisely because the underlying pattern of stuff was so different.

There is no harm, as Professor Robbins pointed out long ago[2] (when he warned against the dangers inherent in the use of aggregates to portray social income), in conventional ways of looking at certain things. The danger arises when we forget what is convention and what is reality, and when merely conventional symbolism determines unduly the goals of public policy.

Perhaps after all it is time for some searching questions about the significance of the Nature and Content of, and Variations in, the *real pattern of welfare* in different societies rather than about the mental fictions which are alleged to symbolize it.

---

[1] Alfred Marshall, *Principles of Economics*, 8th edition, p. 130, referred to by Scitovsky.
[2] *An Essay on the Nature and Significance of Economic Science* (1932).

ESSAY IV

SOME ASPECTS OF INTERNATIONAL ECONOMIC DEVELOPMENT OF UNDER-DEVELOPED TERRITORIES

I. Introduction

MANY attempts have been made to define an 'under-developed' country, region or community. All the definitions known to me leave much to be desired. The difficulty consists in the fact that while development is not necessarily a measurable it is always an evolutionary process; while the forms or symbols under which it is subsumed frequently remain, or appear to remain, the same, the ' realities ' to which they correspond are altered.

Indeed, to speak of development, or lack of it, at all, is to assume that the society to which the term is applied is proceeding, or is failing to proceed, in a certain direction —towards a preconceived foreseeable goal or end, the attainment, or partial attainment, of which will indicate a more desirable state of affairs than that now being experienced, or than that which the society experienced in the past. In other words, to speak of the process of development is to assume, or imply, consciously or unconsciously, certain standards or criteria of such development.

Whether a society is regarded as economically developed or under-developed will depend, therefore, on the specific criteria of development applied by the observer, and the position occupied by him. They will vary according to whether the observers are within or outside the society ; whether they are or are not also actors in it ; whether they comprise the whole, a large, or a small part of it ; whether they apply criteria based on their own experience, or criteria borrowed from others; whether such criteria are based on the past, or rest on utopian conceptions of the unrevealed future ; whether they appeal to the reason or judgment, or the whims or appetites of their fellow men ; whether to the ' lessons of history ' or, like the prophets of old, to transcendental values and the word of God.

As Schumpeter wrote about capitalism, it is well to remember that the fate of a particular society ' is not a question of the merits or demerits we may individually see in it. Our judgment about these is a matter of personal or groupwise preference that depends on interests and ideals largely determined by our personal or groupwise location in the social organism. What we mean when we say that we are for or against capitalism ' (or as I here suggest ' for or against ' a particular stage of economic development) ' is that we like or dislike a certain civilization or scheme of life. . . . But civilizations are incommensurable. Even if we agreed to neglect those cultural aspects, which are what really matters to us, and to make the " desirability " of retaining or eliminating capitalism turn on some purely economic criterion—such as comparative productive efficiency—we should never agree about the result. For even if those extra-economic and largely extra-rational preferences did not prevent us from admitting that any criterion could ever tell against the alternative we have chosen to espouse—which they no doubt would in most cases—we should immediately challenge a criterion that did. No amount of honest intention to place oneself on the standpoint of the public welfare or of the nation's interest avails against that. For the point is precisely that these words carry different meanings for different minds. The only thing we can do in something like a scientific frame of mind is therefore to try to visualize, irrespective of our wishes, the actual situations which may be expected to emerge and the relative power of the groups which will be in a position to assert their interests and ideals in handling those situations.'[1]

But let us not forget that history is the record of social action not of passive observation. Indeed, the belief (which I do not share)[2] that development is merely a ' rational ' process of social choice and hence that it is above all a question of social *will*, and determinate action based thereon, lies at the root of the outlook of the modern Western world. The history of social development—development as social history

---

[1] Joseph A. Schumpeter : ' Capitalism in the Post War World ' in *Postwar Economic Problems*, edited by Seymour E. Harris, McGraw-Hill Book Company, Inc., 1943, p. 113. Quoted with permission of the publisher.
[2] I am not here concerned with either the validity or the philosophical implications of that belief.

—is the story of the ambivalent role of man in search of freedom to choose the ends of action and of conscious or unconscious desires to impose those ends on others, or have them imposed upon himself—either for what he believes consciously or unconsciously to be for his sake or for theirs ; either out of conviction that he *knows* or has had revealed to him what is good for them, or as a rationalization for what he rightly or wrongly conceives to be good for himself.

II. 'INCOME AGGREGATES' AS CRITERIA OF INVESTMENT AND DEVELOPMENT

It is of importance to probe behind the symbolisms in which the criteria of development we consciously, or unconsciously, apply are clothed.

It is clearly not possible within the compass of this essay to examine the many different criteria of development which have been suggested or of the large number (many of them contradictory in themselves),[1] that have been made use of by

[1] For a critical analysis of current criteria of development I would refer the reader to Professor Jacob Viner's 'International Trade and Economic Development,' The Free Press, Glencoe, Illinois, 1952. I would draw particular attention to the following challenging statement in Lecture VI (pp. 126–127). 'Let us suppose, for instance,' writes Professor Viner, 'that a country which has embarked on a program of economic development engages in periodic stock-taking of its progress, and finds not only that aggregate wealth, aggregate income, total population, total production, are all increasing, but that per capita wealth, income, production, are also increasing. All of these are favourable indices, but even in combination do they suffice to show that there has been " economic progress ", an increase in economic " welfare ", rather than retrogression?

' Suppose that someone should argue that the one great economic evil is the prevalence of a great mass of crushing poverty, and that it is a paradox to claim that a country is achieving economic progress as long as the absolute extent of such poverty prevailing in that country has not lessened or has even increased? Such a country, nevertheless, might be able to meet all the tests of economic development which I have just enumerated. If its population has undergone substantial increase, the numbers of those living at the margin of subsistence or below, illiterate, diseased, undernourished, may have grown steadily consistently with a rise in the average income of the population as a whole. . . .

' . . . Were I to insist, however, that the reduction of mass poverty be made a crucial test of the realization of economic development, I would be separating myself from the whole body of literature in this field. In all the literature on economic development I have seen, I have not found a single instance where statistical data in terms of aggregates and of averages have not been treated as providing adequate tests of the degree of achievement of economic development. I know, moreover, of no country which regards itself as underdeveloped which provides itself with the statistical data necessary for the discovery of whether or not growth in aggregate national wealth and in per capita income are associated with decrease in the absolute or even relative extent, to which crushing poverty prevails.'

national and international agencies. What I shall attempt here has a more modest aim. It is to examine some conceptual and praxiological aspects of *investment*, and particularly foreign investment, as a means of furthering the development of ' underdeveloped societies '. Underlying nearly all current discussions of this problem are two assumptions : (*a*) that international policy should be directed to raising the income per capita of the inhabitants of under-developed societies, and (*b*) that one of the main pre-requisites for doing this is to stimulate investment from abroad in them.

These assumptions may or may not be correct. But this is not a matter with which I am immediately concerned. What I am concerned with is the basic implication that low or high ' incomes ' per capita or low or high aggregate ' incomes ' do in fact provide *criteria* for investment policy in relation to ' underdeveloped territories ' at all. I believe it is significant that the current literature on the relation between aggregate ' income ' and investment makes use of terms like gross or net national ' income ' per head *as if* the word ' income ' in such expressions has a similar connotation as a guide for investment decisions as it has, or had, in a money-exchange economy for a private entrepreneur or promoter. In other words, it uses aggregate ' income ' as an accounting symbol and as a rationale for economic policy.

It is I believe basic to the problems considered in this essay to realize that the ' income ' criterion of investment applied by a private entrepreneur has little in common with the use of national, regional, or other collective income aggregates as criteria of investment and social action. In using the term entrepreneurial investment I mean the placing of capital at risk in order to obtain a net monetary return or, more exactly, a net increase in the value of the capital which increase can be converted into money. The rationale of private or ' business ' investment, i.e. the investment of money made by the entrepreneur or a ' legal ' entity acting as such (and independent within the field of action for which it has been set up), is made with the sole object of deriving an income or profit from that investment in an accounting sense. Such income, or profit, or monetary return, consists in the net *increase* in the value of the capital and is nothing other than this in so far as the entrepreneur is concerned. In fact strictly speaking there is no such thing as a *flow* of income from an investment of capital. The income arises from the increase in the *value* of the assets and their disposal (in whole or part) from time to time.

Capital and income are—as Irving Fisher stressed long ago—logically exclusive terms;[1] when income is received by the investor he must decrease his capital to an equal extent. Income thus represents a ' decrease ' of the capital value attained at that time—an exchange of that portion of the capital, which is ' detached ' from it, for money or for a money equivalent.[2]

Moreover, the use of these ' income ' aggregates *as if* they were automatic and trustworthy criteria of development and investment policy overlooks the fact that these aggregates are only statistical estimates of events which lie wholly in the past : they are abstractions which cannot serve as a guide to future action. They are therefore not adequate criteria of *calculation*. To say, for example, that more investment is required to increase the ' aggregate income ' of a society is like saying that we must spend more money in order ' to cure disease '. ' To cure disease ' is a laudable slogan not a specific objective ; it cannot fulfil the requirements of a criterion of action. It is not a possible criterion of action because it does not tell us what ' disease ' consists in. Moreover it does not tell us which of the many alleged or real diseases shall (or shall not) be cured, and at what cost, e.g. whether *at the expense* of better housing (which might prevent some ' disease ') ; or at the expense of old-age pensions which might keep old people alive longer ; or at the expense of food subsidies to reduce the infantile death rate ; or at the expense of ' defence ' to safeguard the whole population against its neighbours ; or at the expense of agricultural

---

[1] Cf. Essay No. III in this volume.

[2] Thus to say that an investor who invests capital in buying house 'A' rather than house ' B ' although both houses cost the same, have the same market value, and yield the same net money income, is obtaining an additional ' income ' because he has what he thinks is a better view from 'A' than from ' B ' is not a correct use of the word ' income '. Such ' subjective ' income is not ' income ' in an accounting sense. Whatever its importance it has no relevance to the pure act of private investment for which the basic criterion is the achievement of a net increase in the value of the capital which increase can if desired be ' detached ', i.e. exchanged for money.

research to protect its food supply against the ravages of insect-born pests. To argue that capital investment is required in an under-developed country to increase the ' aggregate incomes ' of the population is to postulate a similarly impracticable criterion of action. To use the word ' income ' to describe abstract collective aggregates is to overlook the fact that in a society in which ' income ' is increasing, the goods and services which compose that ' income ' must be changing.

As Professor Mises has so well expressed the matter : ' The impracticability of measurement is not due to the lack of technical methods for the establishment of measure. It is due to the absence of constant relations. If it were only caused by technical insufficiency, at least an approximate estimation would be possible in some cases. But the main fact is that there are no constant relations. Economics is not, as ignorant positivists repeat again and again, backward because it is not ' quantitative '. It is not quantitative and does not measure because there are no constants. Statistical figures referring to economic events are historical data. They tell us what happened in a non-repeatable historical case. Physical events can be interpreted on the ground of our knowledge concerning constant relations established by experiments. Historical events are not open to such an interpretation.'[1]

The point is that if we *assume* that there is *agreement* on what additional ' incomes ' are to be produced and in what form ; if we assume further that the type, nature and extent of ' investment ' which will produce them is known in advance ; if we assume there will be no changes of any kind in the future which can obviate this knowledge ; if we assume that the future additional incomes (i.e. the future growth of capital) are an automatic consequence of the additional capital investment, and that it is known precisely how much of the additional income can be detached from capital so as not to impair the ' original ' value of the latter ; if we assume, finally, that the idea of *aggregate national capital* and its increase in ' value ' is a meaningful concept at all, then

[1] Ludwig von Mises : *Human Action—A Treatise on Economics*, Yale University Press, 1949, p. 56. Quoted with permission of the publisher.

indeed the use of increases or decreases in aggregate incomes as a criterion of development is justified—but then, I submit, our knowledge is so perfectly attuned to the infinite future that the problem has been assumed away.

To those who would care to make these assumptions somewhat haphazardly I would only suggest that a study of the range of possible conflicts as to the purpose of ' investment ', the direction that ' increases in aggregate incomes ' should take, and of the ' uncertainties ' which in the real world encompass the growth of capital (and therefore of income) might prove salutary. They are illustrated currently by events in Iran, or historically by the attitude of President Kruger to the ' uitlanders ' who wanted to ' develop ' gold-mining in the Transvaal, or by the experience of the Overseas Food Corporation, set up by the British Government, in choosing to ' develop ' ground-nut [peanut] cultivation in an unsuitable area in Tanganyika[1] chosen partly in order to obviate the need to move elsewhere Africans who were engaged in ' subsistence ' production on what would have been the better land for the project.

But I must return to the main point of this analysis. It is designed to show that where there are contradictory objectives of policy, where the ends of action or goals of endeavour are not, at least symbolically, assumed to be relatively clear cut —at any rate for the actor on the social scene—there can be no specific calculation at all. Vague and necessarily conflicting objectives such as are conveniently obscured by statistical aggregates of the type we have been discussing cannot be used as criteria of ' calculation '—except by an authoritarian state which sets its own goals of action irrespective of the costs thereof to the human agents through which they are pursued.

III. The Criterion of Private Investment

The criterion of private investment as an economic activity is, and continues to be (in so far as it is not affected by changes in legal and fiscal institutions and practices), the ' marginal efficiency ' of the capital in the basic sense, and in that sense only, that the ' efficiency ' is expressed as ' income ' which is recorded in accounting transactions. Such income

[1] Cf. Essay No. VIII in this volume.

accrues through changes expressed in the ' market ' valuation of the capital assets at risk.

In the historic nineteenth century development of the ' world-economy ', in which Britain played the role of ' The World's Banker ', the basic characteristic of the domestic and foreign investment situation consisted in the fact *that as far as the investor was concerned he was, and in the exercise of his function was supposed to be,* concerned only with the problem of so choosing the direction of his investment, and so embarking his capital, as to obtain the relatively highest net income therefrom over comparable periods of time and in comparable circumstances. This objective was the fly-wheel of investment activity. That it was so is not in the least invalidated by the fact that various European governments endeavoured, and were able, by propaganda, subtle political pressures, controls and economic devices to skew the judgment of, and to reduce the opportunities open to, investors to direct investments into the channels they would otherwise have chosen. One need only mention the extensive loans raised for Russia on the French capital market, or the diversion of British capital to the British Colonies and Dominions through the operation of the Colonial Stock Acts ; these gave trustee status to Empire Bonds which latter would otherwise have not proved as attractive to the functional calculations of the investor.

All that this shows is that the European states were, or thought they were, justified in interfering with the established market criterion in order to achieve other objectives for ' national ' reasons ; and were applying, or thought they were applying, other criteria of investment.

The contrast between what to the investor or, indeed, to any entrepreneur, appears as a clear-cut accounting symbolism or criterion of action and other non-market criteria is of great significance. Much confusion has resulted from the fact that even eminent economists have frequently used arguments based on a sudden shift from one set of criteria to another. Thus Mr. J. M. Keynes in a significant article, written long before the Second World War,[1] criticized the Colonial Stock

---

[1] ' Foreign Investment and National Advantage ' by J. M. Keynes. *The Nation and the Athenaeum,* August 9, 1924, pp. 985–986.

'A considerable proportion of the growing wealth of the community accrues in the hands of individuals or of corporations which by law or by strong custom and con-

Acts because they in effect compelled investment abroad which might otherwise, he thought, have been utilized at home. ' It follows from this ' wrote Keynes, ' that large sums may flow abroad without there having been a *vestige of deliberate calculation on the part of anybody that this is the best way of employing* the resources in the national interest.'[1]

But significantly he did not indicate anywhere, either in this or subsequent writings, as far as I am aware, how such a calculation could be made. He was, however, very critical of the criteria of calculation which had led to the private investments of the nineteenth century. 'In short', he wrote, ' the nineteenth century, as in so many other respects, came to look on an arrangement as normal which was really most abnormal. To lend vast sums abroad for long periods of time without any possibility of legal redress, if things go wrong, is a crazy construction ; especially in return for a trifling extra interest.' This may well be so, but in adopting this argument Keynes has shifted the discussion on to an entirely different plane. He is no longer discussing the obstacles to the application of those accounting criteria of calculation which are necessarily utilized by the investor acting functionally in the investment market, he is throwing those criteria overboard altogether. Thus he wrote : ' Consider two investments, the one at home and the other abroad, with equal risks of repudiation or confiscation or legislation restricting profit. It is a matter of indifference to the individual investor which he selects. But the nation as a whole retains in the one case the object of the investment and the fruits of

vention, are compelled to invest the whole or the bulk of it in the Trustee group of securities. They are limited in their choice to what securities are available within this group. It follows that if, in any year, there is no net increase in the amount of home Trustee stocks, the *whole* of the annual increased savings available for investment in this form is *compelled* to go abroad. If, by reason of the repayment of Government debt, there is actually a decrease in the available home securities, the compulsion to invest abroad is even more stringent.

' Incidentally it is worth noting that to pay off our own Government debt out of the proceeds of taxation, without at the same time providing a supply of home Trustee investments to take its place, involves taking money by taxation out of the hands of persons who might invest in home enterprises of a non-Trustee type and transferring it to another type of person who cannot help investing the proceeds in Trustee investments abroad.' (Quoted with the permission of the *New Statesmen and Nation.*) It is of interest, in passing, to contrast this complaint of Keynes with what is now quite normal practice viz. the taking of money directly by taxation and its ' investment ' abroad.

[1] Italics not in the original

it ; whilst in the other case both are lost. If a loan to improve a South American capital is repudiated we have nothing. If a Poplar housing loan is repudiated, we, as a nation, still have the houses. If the Grand Trunk Railway of Canada fails its shareholders by reason of legal restriction of the rates chargeable or for any other cause, we have nothing. If the Underground System of London fails its shareholders, Londoners still have their Underground System.'

This argument misses the essential basis of international investment in the nineteenth century, namely that it was by and large, and notwithstanding frictions and political interferences, conducted on the implicit assumption that for investment purposes the world-economy of the Great Powers and their peripheral and colonial dependencies were one, and should be regarded as one. And in fact it did function broadly as a unity ; there did come about an international division of labour and investment which was less influenced by deliberate political and economic barriers than at any time before or after this unique period. To put the matter more forcibly, the arguments advanced by Keynes that it was absurd to invest in the Grand Trunk Railway, even if the index of profitability indicated that it was more desirable than an investment in the Underground System of London, would at that time have been regarded as absurd, because the London Underground was thought of as serving a Metropolis of the world, rather than the capital of yet another little national state. London it might well have been argued might not have required an Underground System, if it had remained the capital of ' a little England,' just as it may no longer be able to afford those ' houses in Poplar ' should it again be forced to become one.

Arguments concerned with the alleged ' national advantage or disadvantage ' of foreign investment, just like the endless discussion about whether colonies ' pay ', and the attempts to draw up a ' Balance Sheet of Imperialism ' are not based on, and cannot be considered as if they were based on, *investment* criteria. Such arguments involve discussion on two different planes or categories of thought : discussion about the ' profitability ' of *investment* assumes a common accounting standard or symbolism, whereas discussion about national

F

advantage or disadvantage denies it. A ' colony ' cannot be said to pay the ' colonizing power ' as an investment is said to ' pay ' an investor : any more than one would argue that i ' pays ' New York to bring about the economic development of New England, or that it ' paid ' London to bring about the development of India. Such developments represent the growth, or extension of one ' market '. They were, and are valuable precisely because the development or extension of a single market, in place of separate and disparate ones, brings with it those great economies in the diversification of economic efforts all of which are too well-known to require any elaboration.

If I may anticipate, I would say that when we speak of the ' income ' yielded by an investment in an accounting sense the word ' income ' is used to connote the *same* money or money equivalents as those in which the amount of capital so invested is reckoned. But the moment we speak of foreign investment by ' nation A ' intended to bring about an increase in ' aggregate incomes ' in ' nation B '—the word ' income ' no longer necessarily refers to the same money or money equivalents as are assumed in A. The *private* investor of country A who invests in B is not concerned with this difference, because, as an investor, his accounting is solely in terms of the money-of-account of *his* society, and its own homogeneous system of pricing (assuming the absence of exchange controls, etc.) When, however, ' investment ' is undertaken by the government of country A in order to increase the ' aggregate income of country B the word ' income ' may have a quite different connotation in A from that in B. In other words the investment action is not conducted on the same plane of mutually accepted accounting discourse.[1]

IV. THE ACCUMULATION OF CAPITAL

It is of importance not to regard the calculations of the private entrepreneur in terms of established accounting symbolisms as in any sense an automatic or mechanical process

---

[1] Herein of course lies one of the causes of the well-known ' balance of payments difficulties.' The ' investment ' may yield ' income ' of a type which is not transferable —e.g. of a kind quite different from that which it would have yielded ' at home ' in the lending country where ' income ' is in an accounting sense ' homogeneous ' and of course ' transferable '.

To regard the investment of capital as leading automatically to that net increase in the value of the capital which increase can be detached as ' income ', is a common fallacy. The symbolism of accounting is a device to assist the making of choices ; but no amount of calculation guarantees the result.

The accumulation of capital was never regarded in the nineteenth century, as it now frequently is, as the necessary consequence merely of an ' investment ' decision. The accumulation of capital was not regarded as necessarily consequent upon, and as automatically resulting from the exercise of individual or social *will*. On the contrary, as the common tongue of enterprise clearly shows, the success of ' venture ' capital was regarded, and rightly regarded, as having much to do with ' good fortune ', ' wise-choices ', the correct ' embarking ' of capital in the ' right ' directions, at the ' right ' time. It was seen to be a matter of ' patience ', ' waiting', 'flexibility', 'adaptability', 'experience', 'growth', and as dependent upon the ' character ' of the entrepreneur, his ' intuition ' and ' experience ', his ' connexions', ' good-will ', his courage in meeting ' unforeseen circumstances ', and his ' foresight' in being able to ally himself with the new opportunities, innovations and resources which would yield the ' quasi-rents ' of new endeavours.

Much confusion has resulted from the fact that the large volume of fixed-interest bearing securities issued by modern governments (mainly for purposes of war finance) led to the belief that investment was something which automatically yielded income. Thus it became fashionable to speak as if (and for some apparently even to believe that) capital *neces-sarily generates* income of itself ; both ' capital ' and 'income' came to be regarded as ' abstract', functionally related, entities.

It is in this connexion significant that a large proportion of the overseas investments of the European powers in the pre-1914 era were also in fixed-interest bearing securities.[1]

---

[1] See Sir Arthur Salter's valuable analysis : ' Foreign Investment.' *Essays in International Finance No.* 12. International Finance Section, Princeton University, February 1951 and Herbert Feis, *Europe the World's Banker* 1820–1914. Yale University Press, 1930. See also my *Capital Investment in Africa*, Oxford University Press, 1938, in which I showed that roughly 48 per cent of all British capital invested in Africa was provided by, or guaranteed by, government or semi-government agencies.

In the British Colonies and Dominions these investments were particularly ' successful ' i.e. the service of the debts of governments, municipalities etc. was on the whole regularly met. I think it would warrant careful inquiry as to why this was so. In many cases it is clear that these investments by public authorities in railways, etc. really produced the ' income ' which the investor received. But in many other cases the provision of this ' overhead capital ', as it is nowadays vaguely designated, was in fact *premature* and did not *yield* ' income '. The debt service was met by the *compulsory* raising of revenue by taxation. Often the taxes so raised could not in any way be regarded as having resulted from these premature capital expenditures. Moreover the fact noted by Sir Arthur Salter that ' repayments, particularly of Government borrowing, were normally made out of the proceeds of new loans ' is significant as showing the long period of time required for the capital so invested to yield *net* income. Indeed, the fact that these debts were eventually mostly repaid, without further borrowing abroad, was partly because of the general depreciation of the monetary units in which they were expressed.

The point I wish to stress is that the receipt of income by the foreign investor in cases like this—or in cases in which the debt service was met by subsidy or was borne by the issuing metropolitan government on behalf of the colony— could not be regarded as true income yielded by the investment itself. Yet it is very common nowadays to suggest that the provision of capital in any form is necessarily advantageous to the recipient society and automatically produces ' income '. Nothing could be further from the truth. The history of such ' investments ' in Africa and elsewhere affords many examples of railway lines, roads, ports, irrigation works etc. in the ' wrong places ' which not only failed to lead to income-generating development, but actually inhibited more economic developments which might otherwise have taken place.

In other words a capital export to, or import by, an under-developed country—a capital outlay or input—is not necessarily *investment* at all—it may well represent only capital consumption i.e. its use in situations where it is impossible, or still premature, to expect economic activity sufficient to maintain or replace the capital and provide for its further accumulation.

Capital, it cannot be emphasized too strongly, is, apart from the symbolism of accounting, always ' concrete ' in the sense that it is embedded in, and attuned to, the particular purposes and state of knowledge which led to its ' creation '. It is but temporarily incorporated in ever changing forms and patterns suited to the evanescent ends for which it is designed. It is a social heritage dependent upon the institutions and habit-patterns of thought and action of individuals in society. In the last resort it dissolves always into its basic element : the action of man's labour upon the natural environment. That is why capital cannot be ' stored-up ' for long ; nor can it be ' transferred ' from one situation to another without the individuals who will re-adapt and ' re-fashion ' it for use in a new pattern of activity. For no two situations, no two regions, no two societies, no two problems of choice, in time, or place, are alike. In this sense capital is like technical ' know-how ', which also does not exist in the abstract ready to be applied to any new situation. To transfer 'know-how' is not to apply something which is known. It is to apply new ways of thinking to find out what is not known : as when research is undertaken to develop new crops ; discover the nature of soils ; prospect for minerals ; adapt old aptitudes to new skills ; and perfect machines for new tasks. It is because existing forms in which knowledge i.e. capital, is incorporated are no longer suitable that the old has constantly to be re-fashioned anew in attempts to meet the future. Capital is, as has been said repeatedly, a means of saving time ; but it is only possible to save time if one can discover the purpose to which one will devote it.

The great growth of capital in the eighteenth and nine-teenth centuries in Europe was due not to mechanical forces but to the evolution of new patterns in social relationships. It was due to the emergence of new types of social activity. ' Saving ' was not a mechanical act but the result of new attitudes in social behaviour. To repair and maintain ; to think of to-morrow not only of to-day ; to educate and train one's children ; to prepare oneself for new activities ; to acquire new skills ; to search out new contacts ; to widen the horizon of individual experience ; to invent, to improve, to question the 'dead hand of custom', and the heritage of the past—in all these, and not in mechanical calculations, or mechanical regimentation, lay the causes of capital accumulation. For indeed capital was but 'accumulated' in the ledgers of the counting-house ; in the objective world it was embedded in the general stream of changing activity, in world-wide migration, in the co-operant bonds of commerce and mutual confidence, and in painfully created new aptitudes of action and responsibility.

It is because we have come to think of capital in abstract mechanistic terms that the problem of investment in under-developed countries is frequently so over-simplified. For here indeed we have the very obverse of the picture I have just endeavoured to draw. Here the Western world met with very different patterns of behaviour, and with entirely unknown environmental problems. It met with peoples whose aptitude for that very process of change which underlies the production of capital was little developed, or was inhibited by unsuitable political institutions and ideologies. This made the transmission of Western habits of thought and action an extremely difficult, and a necessarily long drawn out process. In short, the West met with goals of social and individual action quite other than those to which it was accustomed, and therefore took for granted.

V. The 'Dilemma' of Development

If saving in time is the essence of capital, the goal of investment is the essence of calculable action. The Western world was confronted in the peripheral areas of its expanding world-economy, not only with the vast task of economically penetrating, physically harnessing, and politically integrating, those dormant regions, but with the far more difficult, and indeed finally unsolved task, of finding at least a common basis for, and a common language of, individual and social endeavour. That task still continues. But the climate of economic and political opinion and organization has changed. Thus some of the assumptions and criteria on the basis of which investment took place in the nineteenth and twentieth centuries are no longer valid ; others are no longer accepted as valid ; and still others are completely misapprehended, in both the underdeveloped and advanced societies.

What confuses the problem of economic development in our time is not so much a change in the basic pre-requisites of economic growth but a change in dominant attitudes towards it. Let us briefly examine the nature of this change. As I have shown, it was because of the existence of a generally accepted integrating symbolism of common purpose that the private investor in the Western world economy was permitted to conduct his highly decentralized operations in accordance with a calculus of individual action.

Thus the entrepreneur was freed from the necessity to choose between different and therefore necessarily conflicting goals of action. As far as he was concerned the purpose of investment was the production of additional net income. He was not distracted by such questions as whether the pursuit of that accounting objective would or would not bring about an increase in welfare, social efficiency, or happiness.

When he subscribed to a loan for or made a direct investment in an underdeveloped country he, as an investor, was not concerned with whether the loan would have good or bad effects on the welfare, health, or social structure of the borrowers. All such matters were not his responsibility, but were assumed, often indeed all too conveniently assumed, to flow from the hidden hand of providence, given only that each man ' calculated ' correctly in regard to that which it was his responsibility to calculate about.

Thus the very notion of ' developing ' a whole community, a whole people, or an under-developed territory did not arise. What was meant by ' development ' was the creation of political and economic institutions which would bring new regions and other peoples into the accepted framework of reference for economic action.

The role of government in the colonial or dependent peripheral areas was, within the system of thought of the times, therefore, clear-cut and consistent. It was to provide (*a*) political security ; (*b*) due processes of law and incorruptible organs of administration ; (*c*) an adequate fiscal and monetary system ; and (*d*) adequate communications and similar public services. It was always clearly realized that the provision of these pre-requisites was a *costly* responsibility not *lightly* to be embarked upon. As it was beyond the means of the under-developed territories themselves, they had to be *given* appropriate grants or assisted by subsidized investments of the type to which I have already referred.

In this respect the importance of many of the ideas now emphasized in the so-called ' Point Four ' programme were clearly realized. It was, however, not so well understood (and is even now not always clearly grasped) that the provision of the framework of economic expansion is in itself insufficient. It was not realized that in the underdeveloped territories the same symbolism and goals of action which were taken for granted in the metropolitan countries could not be relied upon to supply the flesh and blood of individual action to clothe the skeletal framework which ' opened up ' these areas.

It is not an accident that by and large it was in the ' empty ' peripheral areas (such as Australia, New Zealand, the United States, etc.) that the most economic progress was achieved. These regions received large migrations of peoples from Europe itself—peoples with the same habit patterns of thought, the same symbolism of accounting, the same aptitudes and broadly the same conscious and unconscious social heritage. As de Tocqueville so well expressed it : 'At the period when the peoples of Europe landed in the New World their national characteristics were already completely formed ; each of them had a physiognomy of its own.'

Where, however, there were large indigenous populations with a different social heritage the provision of the Western framework did not by itself stimulate such economic development. It is unfortunately not possible to examine here the many reasons for this failure. I mention it merely to show how facile is the assumption so common in much present-day literature that development necessarily follows automatically upon the investment of foreign capital. If the long arduous history of modern colonization shows anything at all it shows that its success was, in the last resort, due to the millions of *individual migrants* who made the mechanical framework vibrate with new co-operant human action.

Societies, like individuals, unconsciously project their

own view of reality, their own problems and what they conceive to be the ' solutions ' to them, on to others. It is not surprising that just as the Western metropolitan powers in the nineteenth century thought that the problem of development of the peripheral areas would ' solve ' itself within the common framework, so now opinion has swung to the other extreme. It sees the problem of developing the under-developed territories as dependent mainly on the provision of capital with which the governments of politically independent communities can pursue collective economic objectives as they may decide. It assumes that this procedure will lead to the same beneficent consequences as are now frequently expected of it in the ' advanced ' countries.

But just as the nineteenth century expectation of the effects of international *private* investment in under-developed territories was an over-simplification of the basic economic and social difficulties of development in them, so its modern variant of development based on *collective* criteria, and directed by national governments, is in danger of proving equally so. For one of the main reasons why foreign investment was possible at all in the under-developed regions of the nineteenth century world economy was that not only was there *assumed* to be a consistent framework of reference for economic activity, but because everything was done to provide the framework itself.[1]

Although there was in all this no *overt* conflict in basic ideologies I need hardly remind the reader that *covert* conflicts of goals were inevitably intensified *pari passu* with the disintegration of the indigenous societies. Their peoples were drawn in ever-increasing numbers into a new social and economic environment and dissociated from their old social values and ways of life. These became ever more difficult to reconcile with the new economic objectives and system of calculation. For many reasons, which it would require a separate essay to explore, there developed a growing gulf between the objectives of foreign investment and the aspira-

---

[1] For example metropolitan governments pursued economic and fiscal policies designed to make it possible for the territories concerned to meet the service of the debts incurred by them. This is of considerable significance, because governments regarded themselves as in the last resort *dependent* on the capital market for raising loans and not as its master.

tions, or alleged aspirations, of the indigenous peoples. That gulf was not bridged, as had been implicitly assumed would be the case, by the emergence, in sufficient numbers, of a new class of indigenous entrepreneurs, professional and technical workers etc. which it had been expected would ' naturally ' become the bearers of ' economic advance '— in the image of Western social ideologies and symbolisms.

It is precisely at this point that we meet with the basic dilemma facing the governments of under-developed territories and those international agencies concerned to promote international economic development in them. For although the constructive forces of newly emergent nationalisms are very great, and engender new hope, new freedom, and new aspirations, they do not remove the inevitable problems and conflicts necessarily involved in all change. Thus the new independent governments of the peripheral regions of the Western world economy are basically confronted, *vis-à-vis* the people they govern, with those same problems of inducing new forms of economic growth which the Western world failed adequately to solve.

It is upon the shoulders of the new governments that there now rests the heavy burden of reconciling their peoples to the fact that structural and social change is inevitable if the burden of their poverty is to be eased; that the costs of change are heavy ; that the capital therefore is scarce, and that the fruits of it are slow to ripen. It is, in my opinion, doubtful whether in this task these governments are assisted by current political and economic philosophies, which would make it appear that economic growth is not a decentralized process resting on the enterprise of the many, but one solely dependent upon the exercise of wisdom, foresight and power by the few.

Development can be neither foreseen, nor enforced by any single will—be it the ' general will ' or the will of a tyrant. It is but the process of evolving patterns of activity, unfolding in one direction, disappearing in another —as obstacles to it are either removed or cannot be surmounted, and as beliefs, aptitudes, and hopes change. Foreign investment, like all investment, is but a part of that process. It consists in bringing into being new, socially acceptable, patterns of co-operant behaviour. To regard it

merely in terms of the conflict of social or political will is
to apply to it a category of thought in which it cannot be
adequately expressed.

Yet this is precisely the impasse to which we are led by
the view that economic development must be determined by
collective objectives expressed in the symbolism of aggregate
statistical abstractions. All the tensions of change are pro-
ected on to the central authorities who appear to be responsible for them. They in turn project them outwards on to the
plane of international economic and political strategy. Here
the final absurdity of this view of economic growth is exposed :
it now appears to result not from the actions of individual
men and women, but from the success with which the national
economic war of each against all can be conducted.

Thus there has been torn apart even the semblance of
that common economic framework which governed the world
economy, at least in general and symbolic terms, until the end
of the Second World War. In place of the vast network of
continuous decentralized decision, and the mutual relationships
of individual trust based on patiently garnered experience,
we have the relatively clumsy and fitful negotiations of parlia-
ments and governments, whose composition changes as
rapidly as their necessarily inconsistent national objectives.
It is symptomatic of the conflict of objectives that these are
sometimes so far removed from any specific economic purpose
that even the lenders are not always agreed why lending
should be undertaken at all. In this connexion it is surely
significant that the discussion about the amount of capital
which should be made available by the United States for
underdeveloped countries has frequently been based not on
the opportunities actually available for its economic *use* but
on alleged ' calculations ' as to how much the United States
economy *must* ' invest ' abroad (in the aggregate!) to ' maintain ' full employment, export industries etc. at home. It is
equally significant that the borrowers frequently do not even
attempt to base their nationally expressed demands for
capital[1] on any common criteria at all but on a vast range of

---

[1] Not to be confused with ' investment '—since the term ' investment ' implies at
least *some* expectation that the ' capital ' will yield ' income ' and not merely be consumed.

political, social, and economic ' needs ' the relative importance of which it is difficult enough to assess *within* the countries concerned, and well-nigh impossible to evaluate as between the national claimants themselves.[1]

It may well be that the increasing pressure of events resulting from this untenable situation will compel borrowing governments to realize that it is necessary, in their own self-defence against the more utopian demands made upon them, to seek for institutional devices to lead the investment process back into more mundane channels, and that new international measures to safeguard and control decentralized foreign investment within a new common framework of reference will receive support in unexpected quarters.

VI. CONCLUSION

It is because in the last resort the misuse of capital resources is always a loss of alternative opportunities that action which wastes the scarce capital resources of the world is eventually harmful for lenders and borrowers alike.

The problems of the borrowers are not solved by the receipt of capital which leads to the adoption of an economic pattern which is not income-creating or is incapable of relatively permanent integration into the economic structure into which it is imported. Such injections of capital disrupt the existing but do not rebuild new and continuing patterns of economic behaviour. Such capital imports may in certain cases only postpone the need for meeting the real problem of the economy as long as the capital lasts. The problems of the lending countries can also not be solved by perpetuating patterns of behaviour which are socially, psychologically and economically so unstable that the *raison d'être* for the supply of capital comes to consist in little more than the distribution of unearned largesse to others. There is no limit to the

---

[1] In all this it is essential not to overlook the conditions of international conflict, and the urgency of security measures in defence of the free world which lie at the root of many urgent demands for economic ' assistance ' and ' aid '. The amount of such ' help ' from one country to another has never been, and indeed cannot be determined in accordance with any yard-stick of strict accounting. That kind of capital gift or revenue grant must in the last resort be determined by the political and diplomatic aptitudes, wisdom and experience of those concerned with ' defence ' rather than ' opulence '.

demands for 'capital' which will be made by the recipients or prospective recipients of it on these terms; whereas the amount of capital which can be created by any society, however productive, is not similarly infinite.

I can conceive of no more dangerous illusion at the present conjuncture of world affairs than the facile belief that we have 'solved' the problem of capital accumulation, and that the problem is now not how to produce capital but to whom to give it. The truth is that capital is relatively scarcer and 'time' more pressing than perhaps ever before in the context of the world changes with which we are confronted. The uncertainty engendered by the present international disruption and tension; the heavy demands on the world's resources for coping with the aftermath of two world wars; and the cost of defence to ward off the third world war, all reduce the relative amount of capital available for continuous economic growth. Moreover we are experiencing a period of great technical and scientific transition which threatens a large portion of the capital resources and 'social heritage' of both the developed and the under-developed areas of the world with obsolescence. The advance in public hygiene and social medicine by lowering death rates is engendering a vast increase in the population of many regions which, in relation to their existing patterns of economic and social action, are already overpopulated. This further intensifies the demand for capital for new forms and techniques of production.

All these changes expose to view the inadequate amount of administrative experience and skill necessary to cope with the new challenge to man's individual and social ingenuity. It leads to the feeling that 'time' is 'running out'; that it is insufficient to cope with all these problems by 'waiting' for new institutions, new aptitudes, new skills to *grow*. In the last resort this may lead to counsels of despair such as those which urge 'catastrophic' solutions for these problems; which wish to take 'time by the forelock' by 'spending' capital recklessly to stem the tide; and which are even prepared, if capital in material terms is not available, to expend human lives without mercy to 'create' it, quite overlooking that so to degrade man is not a means consistent with the alleged use of capital to uplift him.

Neither the mere ' expenditure ' of capital nor the application of force can solve the real problems of our time. We are faced not with problems of ' spending ' capital but of ' investing ' it in those multitudinous personal and social forms which can grow only in conjunction with the always unique social heritage of different individuals and societies. The problem is, indeed as it always has been, how to ' husband ' resources in the widest sense of the word. It is how to invest those limited supplies of the world's capital so as to ensure that the ' borrower ' of it will put it to use in such directions as will most readily and in the *relatively least period of time* release new capital resources for coping with the problems arising out of the overall scarcity.

The real problem confronting the ' under-developed ' countries of the world is therefore not only how to economize in the use of foreign capital, but how to utilize all capital— the very social indigenous heritage itself—to achieve new goals of social action with the *least* unnecessary or premature social disintegration and disharmony.

There is, as I have already suggested, an alternative to such strict social economy concerned to foster the irritatingly slow but relatively more harmonious changes involved in the *growth* of new human aptitudes, experiences and purposes. It is the alternative which involves the sacrifice of men and women to-day in order to construct rapidly that which it is *hoped, or alleged* will ease the life of *others* to-morrow. The line between ' capital ' as the servant and as the idol of the fuller life is narrower than we are apt to think.

It is the realization that true economic growth is a many-sided individual and social process which I believe is the most important lesson of past attempts to link under-developed territories and peoples into a wider world economy. It consists in the re-fashioning[1] of aptitudes, and beliefs of individuals to give them new freedom in their multitudinous daily tasks—many of them not assessable in accounting or financial terms. Once this is realized we will perhaps hear less of attempts to reduce ' consumption ', increase ' saving ' and *force* home and foreign ' investment ' in underdeveloped societies. The real task is not to force change but to induce it

[1] Cf. Essay No. II in this volume.

in a manner which will be meaningful to the members of the societies it affects.

It is just here that international ' technical assistance ' and similar activities assume fundamental importance.[1] They are likely to be most successful in so far as they are based on the realization that what is involved is the grafting of the new on the old, and in so far as they proceed with unequivocal emphasis on the dignity and rights of the individual *person* and refuse to jettison *him* in the pursuit of abstract goals. But in order that such assistance programmes should make an appreciable impact they must be seen, in the context of the history of all real ' colonization ',[2] as a long, arduous, and continuous task, to which men and women must be dedicated and trained by long experience, as indeed many of the colonial servants of Britain and other colonizing powers have been. That requires the permanent recruitment of personnel, and the development of co-operative bonds and institutions between the ' advanced ' and the underdeveloped countries on an objective basis ; freed from the momentary whims and vicissitudes of political exigencies. It requires that persons and institutions administering such programmes should not be the mere creatures of the state. It requires, indeed, that the programme should not act merely through government or government agencies at all. It should be as widely based as possible, so that new experimentation in social and economic forms can cover an extensive range of continuous endeavour, be it in the field of private, state, or local government enterprise—in rural or in urban activities. But wherever such endeavours may be, and whatever their forms,

[1] In the activities of the international agencies concerned with ' Technical Assistance ' the world is I believe witnessing the emergence of a further development of that ' international civil service ' which in other fields e.g. the World Health Organization, International Labour Office, and the like constitutes perhaps the most constructive political evolution of this otherwise so disruptive century. It behoves us not to distort that new institutional growth by setting ' impossible ' goals of action for it. Those international civil servants who dedicate themselves to the task of creating a new outlook for the free world deserve that we give them objective support in a manner worthy of their calling by ensuring to them the status, the professional independence and the continuity of action required for its proper exercise. Nothing can do more harm to the growth of a new spirit of objective international action than attempts to pervert it to serve irrelevant and passing purposes either by those who provide or those who receive its benefits. Attempts to force them to undertake activities intended to yield only quick results will, when these are not forthcoming, but lead to dangerous disillusionment.

[2] Cf. Essay No. 1 in this volume

what will be perhaps the main factor making for success or failure will be the degree of continuity with which they will be endowed.

This brings us back to the problem of foreign investment in under-developed countries. For here, as I have already hinted, we are faced with precisely the same basic need for a more objective approach to international co-operation. It is as inescapable a requisite for the economical use of scarce capital as it is for the proper use of an international civil service that a new objective attitude to foreign capital should be fostered.

This in my opinion is the real significance of the establishment of, and the experience already gathered by, the International Bank for Reconstruction and Development. It is that once again there must be developed criteria of international investment which can be *independently* applied and *independently put into operation* by appropriate industrial and commercial institutions, freed from the haphazard interference of governmental or national political influences.

The issue here is not that between private and government investment. The issue is, on the one hand, between the supply of capital for purposes chosen in accordance with criteria suited to the enterprise *per se* (and in one region rather than in another in accordance with generally accepted comparative criteria of economy) and on the other hand the supply of capital for purposes which cannot be comparatively assessed at all in economic terms. The issue is further between the supply of capital to ' enterprise ', whether private or public, which is, rather than to enterprise which is not, capable of pursuing a defined economic aim in the sense of being likely to lead to continuous growth capable of yielding recorded net income.

What I am at pains to emphasize is that not only is the revival of private investment desirable, as is generally agreed, but that decisions by international agencies must themselves increasingly be freed from political pressures which make economic criteria of investment impossible to apply, either before, or after, the investment decision is made. Investment involves a continuing process of decision-making—it involves enterprise *per se*, and it involves therefore the recognition of the need for a large variety of institutions able to conduct it according to evolving international law or custom, and free from interference as long as such law or custom is adhered to. Without the human agencies able to conduct continuous economic operations, unhampered by fiscal or other exactions foreign to their purpose, the growth of capital in any form is impossible ; and foreign *investment* becomes a farce however much this may be camouflaged. This is especially true of investment in ' under-developed ' areas where the experience and aptitude for modern enterprise and the fashioning of administrative devices for its social control are so recent.

I believe that it might prove very valuable if institutions like the International Bank were given the opportunity to develop agreed comparative criteria of world investment ; criteria which would be recognized as taking the place of vague demands for action to further every conceivable national objective ; criteria which would be related to specific purposes, and which would be applied continuously as a code of international conduct relating to the investment itself, and recognized by national governments as such.

Thus we are brought to the central issue confronting a distraught world—whether satisfactory basic codes of, and institutions for, trans-national economic action can still be fashioned, or whether the forces of disintegration must continue unchecked.

But if the forces of disintegration are to be checked at all, it is clear that an appreciation of the real nature of economic growth, and the fragile individual basis on which it rests, will be required by all concerned ; by borrowers and lenders alike. It is perhaps time that, instead of the resolve to better the whole world, and the illusion that there is magic in collective protestations of our will and power to do so, we should give new opportunities for objective international co-operation to the unique diversity of experience of the men and women on whose individual actions and social inventiveness civilization, in the last resort, depends.

To those who would protest that collective national symbolisms are the only forms of expression for co-operant human activity still open to man, I would reply in terms of the old African proverb : ' I cannot hear what you are saying, for what you are is thundering in my ears.'

G

ESSAY V

UNITED NATIONS PRIMER FOR DEVELOPMENT

I. Introduction

THIS essay considers the United Nations report on ' Measures for the Economic Development of Under-developed Countries '. We are informed in the preface, by the Secretary-General of the United Nations, that it should be regarded as a counterpart to the earlier report on national and international measures required to achieve full employment in economically more developed countries.[1]

This report was prepared by a group of experts[2] appointed by the Secretary-General after the Economic and Social Council adopted a far-reaching series of recommendations resulting from a discussion of the earlier report. The terms of reference were, by resolution 290 (XI) of the Economic and Social Council, as follows :

' To prepare, in the light of the current world economic situation and of the requirements of economic development, a report on unemployment and under-employment in under-developed countries, and the national and international measures required to reduce such unemployment and under-employment.'

Notwithstanding the extraordinarily wide scope of these formal terms of reference, concerning which I shall have some observations to make at the end of this essay, it is worth

[1] *Measures for the Economic Development of Under-developed Countries*, Report by a Group of Experts appointed by the Secretary-General of the United Nations. Published by the Department of Economic Affairs, United Nations, May 1951. (United Nations Publication Sales No. 1951.II.B2). The earlier report, *National and International Measures for Full Employment*, December 1949 (United Nations Sales No. 1949 II.A.3), was reviewed by Professor Jacob Viner in the August 1950, issue of the *Quarterly Journal of Economics* in an article entitled : ' Full Employment At Whatever Cost.'

[2] The group was composed of Alberto Baltra Cortez, Professor of Economics, National University of Chile ; D. R. Gadgil, Director, Gokhale Institute of Politics and Economics, Poona, India ; George Hakim, Counselor, Legation of Lebanon, Washington, D.C. ; W. Arthur Lewis, Professor of Political Economy, University of Manchester, England ; and Theodore W. Schultz, Chairman, Department of Economics, University of Chicago, U.S.A. At the request of the group, George Hakim served as Chairman.

noting that a resolution of the General Assembly of the United Nations even asked the experts to deal with a vast range of other matters.[1] It is not surprising that the authors of the report could not even attempt to comply with all these further requests.

II. THE CONCEPT OF PROGRESS

The report is a significant document. It is significant of the increasing world concern with the economic condition and problems of what were once the peripheral regions of a closely integrated ' world-economy ' with its centre in Europe. It is significant, because of the problems arising out of the new-found independence of many of these regions, and their sensitivity to the alleged benefits, but not to the short-comings, of the driving forces of nationalism. It is significant of the humanitarian feelings which actuate much of the valuable work being done to grapple with these questions, and which obviously deeply imbued its authors. But it is also significant because of the *unconscious* expression which it gives of the climate of economic opinion in the middle of the twentieth century. Indeed, it is in itself a very interesting case study for economists, political scientists and even for philosophers, of preconceptions which are apparently current not only in the offices of governments, but also in the more cloistered retreats of academicians—preconceptions which seem at times to be developing into something like an ' Official Concept of Progress ' which it would be tempting to examine at length in all its implications ; but considerations of space forbid more than a brief reference.

The authors of the report, true to the spirit of the times, do not appear to have been troubled unduly by any inconvenient difficulties of definition. To them progress is clearly progress ; if it cannot be clearly seen or sensed (and reading

[1] Namely ' (i) Ways and means of preventing any aggravation of the problems of unemployment and under-employment in under-developed countries that may occur as a result of the mechanization of production in certain branches of industry and agriculture.

' (ii) Measures of social security designed to ensure that there will be no interruption in the income of workers temporarily unemployed through mechanization or technological progress, taking into account the work of the International Labour Organisation in this field.' The authors did not specifically deal with (ii) and, as was to be expected, only cursorily with (i).

the report one almost gets the feeling that it really can be), it can, at any rate, be *measured* in terms of national income aggregates or averages and the like, to which I refer later.

'Economic Progress,' the report states roundly, 'will not occur unless the atmosphere is favourable to it. The people of a country must desire progress, and their social, economic, legal and political institutions must be favourable to it.' (Par. 23).

Therefore ' Economic progress will not be desired in a community where the people do not realise that progress is possible. Progress occurs only where people believe that man can, by conscious effort, *master* nature.'[1] (Par. 24). We are informed that ' This is a lesson which the human mind has been a long time learning. Where it has been learnt, human beings are experimental in their attitude to material techniques, to social institutions, and so on.'

One would have thought that the history of all civilizations has been the history of empirical experimentation in terms of the beliefs and knowledge of their time. The important point at issue, however, is the rate, and the cost—in terms of human life and suffering—at which the process of ' experimentation ' (in itself a very significant abstraction) is being conducted. Here any mechanical notion of progress which presents the issue as merely one of ' mastering nature ' is apt to prove misleading. There are very important reasons why some societies have often experienced long periods in which they found it more economic, or otherwise necessary, to lay stress on adapting themselves to, and working *through* nature, rather than *mastering* it. But nowadays it is not to be expected that such questions will arouse much interest.

More controversial, however, is the emphatic statement (par. 39) that ' Economic progress depends to a large extent upon the adoption by *governments* of appropriate administrative and legislative action, both in the public and private sectors.' This is also a reflection of current opinion, and, in particular, of the belief that development is largely a matter of social *will*. The report offers no evidence in support of this belief; nor does it examine its consequences. It seems to me very

---

[1] Italics in the quotations from the report are not in the original unless specifically so stated.

doubtful whether a history of economic change, of innovation, or of economic growth in different societies supports this optimistic view of the role and capacities of governments. That the authors should so readily adopt it is in itself somewhat strange because of the excellent discussion in Chapter V of the social and traditional obstacles to the introduction of new techniques in under-developed societies. One would have thought that a more careful consideration of the 'irrational' elements in social organization might have led the authors to a less mechanistic concept of development. As it is we are left with the *ex cathedra* conclusion (par. 38) that ' there cannot be rapid economic progress unless the *leaders* of a country at all levels—politicians, teachers, engineers, business leaders, trade-unionists, priests, journalists—desire economic progress for the country, *and are willing to pay its price*, which is the creation of a society from which economic, political and social privileges have been eliminated. On the other hand, *given leadership* and the *public will to advance*, *all problems of economic development are soluble.*' And, as if this were not clear enough, the authors add : ' *We wish to emphasize that the masses of the people take their cue from those who are in authority over them.* If the *leaders* are reactionary, selfish and corrupt, the masses in turn are dispirited, and *seem* to lack initiative. But if the *leaders* win the confidence of the country, and prove themselves to be vigorous in eradicating privilege and gross inequalities, they can inspire the masses with an enthusiasm for progress which carries all before it.' The authors do not dilate on the inconvenient problem of how privilege is to be divorced from *leadership*, but the authoritarian ring of their admonitions should not really be as astonishing to the reader as it may appear to him at first glance. A philosophy which assumes that ' progress ' is mainly a matter of ' public *will*,' and that ' *all problems of economic development are soluble* ', is not likely to find much room for the uniqueness of the potential contribution of the mere individual. In the last resort such a philosophy can hardly avoid the conclusion that the absence of progress must be the fault of ' *the leaders*'. As the individual is but one of the masses (who are to take their ' cue ' from the leaders) he cannot be blamed—while blame on somebody there must be because progress is assumed to be the necessary consequence of somebody *willing* it with sufficient intensity and enthusiasm. It would have been useful to have been told more exactly what the authors meant by ' *willingness to pay the price of economic progress* '. Is it to be paid by the masses or by the leaders, by the young or the old, by the weak or the strong? But, perhaps, other questions were uppermost in their minds, such as those indicated in paragraph 37, where they state : ' In our judgement, there are a number of under-developed countries where the concentration of economic and political power in the hands of a small class, whose main interest is the preservation of its own wealth and privileges, rules out the prospect of much economic progress until a social revolution has effected a shift in the distribution of income and power.' However, it is necessary to turn to other matters.

III.   The Cure for Unemployment

It will be remembered that the terms of reference required a report on national and international measures to reduce unemployment and under-employment in under-developed countries. But the title of the report actually signed by the authors does not include any reference to these questions. Instead it refers to ' measures for the economic development of under-developed countries '.

The reason for this change of emphasis is of considerable theoretical interest. In paragraph 2 the authors state : ' We have had some difficulty in interpreting the terms " under-developed countries " '. Without further discussion, they continue : ' We use it to mean countries in which *per capita real income* is low when compared with the *per capita real incomes* of the United States of America, Canada, Australasia and Western Europe. In this sense, an adequate synonym would be "poor countries" '. Thus under-developed countries are poor countries because they are under-developed, and they are poor (and therefore under-developed), because certain statistics of per capita income tell us that this is so. There remains the difficulty (which is designated as ' theoretical ' by the authors), that it is possible that ' a country be poor because its resources are poor, and in spite of the resources which it has being as fully developed as current knowledge permits '. This, it should be noted, could be an unfortunate obstacle to the main thesis of the report because clearly it would greatly weaken the effectiveness of the ' public will ' to progress and development. But the hurdle is easily cleared by denying its existence in practice, and by the admonition that for the time being we can *all* do better than we are doing anyway. Thus the authors state : ' We have been able to ignore this theoretical difficulty *because we do not believe that there are any such countries.* We certainly do not hold the view that all countries are capable of reaching the same level of per capita production ; differences in the resources of different countries are a real factor in differences of per capita income. On the other hand we believe that, whatever their resources may be, all countries are currently in a position where their national incomes could be greatly increased by better utilization of what they have.' (Par. 3.) This argument somehow, perhaps irreverently, brought to my mind George Orwell's *Animal Farm* with its well-known slogan : 'All animals are equal but some animals are more equal than others.'

The way was now clear for the authors to jettison the main, and so troublesome, question which the terms of reference laid upon them, namely the problem of unemployment and under-employment in under-developed countries. Chapter II, covering only a little over four pages, purports to deal with this question. Unfortunately it contains only a vague, and, I fear, unhelpful account of four categories of unemployment—' cyclical ', ' seasonal ', ' technological ', and ' disguised '. It contains no new material and no specific theoretical analysis of either the extent, or the *nature*, of unemployment or under-employment in under-developed countries. It quotes (par. 20) certain vague estimates of agricultural surplus population in South-eastern Europe, Southern Italy, and Egypt. In the first study quoted ' agricultural surplus population was defined as the number of people engaged in agriculture (active and dependents) who, in any given conditions of agricultural production, could be *removed* from the land without reducing agricultural output '. But agricultural ' output ' and agricultural *net* income are not synonymous terms ; and the mere ' removal ' of persons from the land does not necessarily raise either national net productivity or net national income. It would have been valuable to have had a theoretical analysis of the nature of this process of 'removing' persons from the land, and an assessment or consideration of the great direct and indirect social costs (such as those of urbanization) involved therein. Instead of dealing adequately with this matter, and notwithstanding the fact that the real nature and extent of 'under-employment' have not been established, the report comes to the purely tautologous conclusion that '*the main remedy for under-unemployment is to create new employment opportunities*'. It continues (par. 21) 'Where more land can be brought into cultivation, this will afford some relief. But, in most countries where under-employment is acute, nearly all the cultivable land is already cultivated. Effort has then to be concentrated upon creating new industries off the land, of which manufacturing industries comprise the largest and usually the most promising category. Thus, *the most urgent problem of these countries is industrialization*.'

I must confess that I find this statement difficult to understand. Even taken literally it is certainly not true of very large parts of Africa. But what is the economic connotation of the word 'cultivated'? The real point at issue is the economic effectiveness with which the 'cultivation' is conducted. The implication (in the above passage) that the economic limit to better or more intensive methods of agricultural production has been reached 'in most countries' is not warranted; nor is the jump to the theoretically and factually unsupported conclusion that 'effort has then to be concentrated upon creating new industries off the land'. The authors deal further with this point in paragraphs 187 and 188. In order to avoid misunderstanding I will quote them in full, as follows :

187. In a country where there is no surplus labour, industrialization waits upon agricultural improvement, because industry should receive only those persons whose labour is no longer required in the production of food. The improvement of agriculture and the development of industry thus go hand in hand, but there is nevertheless an important sense in which the former is of prior urgency.

188. The reverse is the case in a country where population is so large in relation to cultivable land, that the land is carrying more people than

can be fully employed in agriculture. In such a situation, technical changes which reduce the number of people required per acre are of no value; investment in agricultural machinery, for example, would be wasteful, except in so far as it enables new lands to be cultivated which could not otherwise be used. Technical changes which increase yield per acre are still of the greatest importance, since in such countries yields are usually so low that the population lives on a very low level of subsistence. But it is frequently found that substantial technical progress in agriculture is not possible without reducing the numbers engaged in agriculture. In this case, a programme of agricultural improvement has to start by developing manufacturing industries which will absorb the surplus population of agriculture. In some under-developed countries, especially in Asia, the development of manufacturing industry is for this reason, apart from others, of the highest priority.

I regard the argument in these paragraphs as fallacious, although at times the conclusion reached may happen to be correct in particular cases. The argument is conducted on the basis of economic *quantities* and not, as it should be, in relation to the production of economic *values*, and a study of their relations. Thus in paragraph 187, where it is assumed that there is no ' surplus ' labour (the word ' surplus ' is again not adequately defined), it is argued that improvement of agriculture is of prior urgency because industry should receive *only* those persons whose labour is no longer required in the production of ' *food* '. But what if industry (e.g., for export) is so productive of economic *values* that ' food ' can be imported in exchange more cheaply than it can be produced at home? In paragraph 188 (the reverse case) the argument again, I submit, leads to a fallacious conclusion. In this case, where population is large in relation to cultivable land, it is argued that the land is carrying more people than can be fully employed in agriculture. It is stated that technical changes which increase yield per acre, though of the greatest importance, are frequently found to reduce the *number* engaged in agriculture. The conclusion is put forward, therefore, that a programme of agricultural improvement has to *start* by developing manufacturing industries which will absorb the ' surplus ' population of agriculture. But the question is left unanswered as to who will then purchase the industrial products. Quite apart from this practical consideration, the argument is fallacious because an intensification of agricultural production might make it possible to build up large export industries resulting in greatly increased incomes ; by so raising productivity in agriculture a market might be created for an organic evolution of manufacturing industry. The real point is that the problem is insoluble in terms of *quantities* of the factors of production, e.g., *numbers* of population, *amounts* of land, *physical yields*, and *quantities* of product.

The inconvenient unemployment problem is finally disposed of in paragraph 22 which concludes : ' new employment must be created *rapidly*. This is the task of economic development. And *this is the reason why the emphasis of our report is upon economic development rather than upon unemployment.*'

The sketchy treatment of the subject in Chapter II did not, however, prevent the authors from including as one of their formal recommendations (page 93, Recommendation No. 4), designed ' to provide the preconditions and institutional framework of economic development ', that ' the government of an under-developed country should *survey the prospects* of creating new productive employment by industrialization, by bringing more land under cultivation, by developing mineral resources, *or by other means* ; and *announce* its programmes for expanding employment '. This is about as useful advice as would be that of a doctor to a patient to the effect that he may be suffering from an *undefined* disease, and that he should therefore take any steps *he* thinks fit to cure it *rapidly* ; but that, above all, he should not fail to announce publicly what he is doing about it.

The basic argument of the report therefore can be summed up as follows : (1) Under-developed countries are poor countries. (2) To ' develop ' them is to make them less ' poor '. (3) When they are less ' poor ', i.e. ' developed ', they will not exhibit the same amount of technological or disguised unemployment. Therefore the cure for unemployment or under-employment is *rapid* economic development. Therefore study of the *nature* of unemployment in under-developed societies is not necessary and the task of the inquiry can be concentrated on how *rapid*[1] economic

---

[1] It should be noted that the word *rapid* is not introduced haphazardly by the authors. It is deliberately and insistently used, and is a keynote of the whole report. Thus in par. 16 it is stated : ' rapid economic development is paradoxically the greatest *cause of* and the greatest *cure for* technological unemployment ' ; and in par. 17 we are told that ' rapid economic development is also the *only* fundamental remedy for *disguised* unemployment.'

development can be brought about, and how it can be financed.

Furthermore as I have shown in the previous two essays, the very idea of development as merely an increase in per capita income is misleading precisely because the concept of income is meaningless without implicit assumptions concerning what income consists in. Thus to say that the object of ' development ' is to achieve ' higher per capita incomes ' is in itself also meaningless. It is as meaningless as saying that development is desirable because it is not desirable that societies should be 'under-developed'—without defining the nature of development itself.

It is significant that although the report began by emphasizing the need for increasing per capita incomes as a means of curing the poverty of poor (i.e. 'under-developed') countries, it nowhere shows how the objective of higher per capita incomes is to be applied as a criterion of policy. In the last resort, the only way of using ' aggregate income ' as a guide to ' development ' is to presuppose some type of ' authoritarian ' decision by somebody or other who will ' dictate ' what these ' incomes ' are to consist in—i.e., what will, and what will not, be permitted to be ' developed ' in order to increase what is then called ' income '. It is, therefore, not surprising to find that two chapters (VIII and IX) of the report are devoted to Development Planning, Priorities and Techniques.

IV. DEVELOPMENT PLANNING

As ' no two countries are exactly alike in their resources or their development potentialities,' state the authors in paragraph 151, ' it will easily be seen that no simple generalizations can be set out to act as concrete guides to development planning. *Those who are responsible* must *soak themselves* thoroughly in the facts of each particular case *and must then use their best judgement* as to what will be the most desirable directions of movement '. It is clear from the report that ' those who are responsible ' are the ' leaders ', ' the government ', etc. Moreover, it is significant that although the authors in various places support the need for private enterprise they are preoccupied with government regulations in regard to it.

Indeed, the words 'individual effort' are sometimes used in a very unusual sense. For example paragraph 220 states : 'One of the most difficult problems connected with the planning and directing of economic activity is the tendency towards excessive centralization which discourages *individual effort*. The only way of meeting this is to be on one's guard constantly and to ensure that the political and economic *planning mechanism* provide the fullest scope, at each stage, for *individual* and *local participation* . . . the preparation of plans and the determination of goals should be affected by a process of building up from local and regional proposals . . .' Thus 'individual effort' does not here mean individual enterprise but the share of the individual in the process of planning.

The tendency to regard development of under-developed countries as the function of planners engaged in a kind of intellectual exercise pervades the whole report.[1] Thus, in paragraph 148, the authors state dogmatically : 'Economic analysis provides two general principles for the use of resources. One is the marginal principle. Resources should be used in such a way that a transfer of marginal units from one use to another could not increase welfare'. 'Welfare' is not defined, and its relation to per capita incomes is not discussed, but the authors continue : '*This tautology is simple and evident ; nevertheless, it is frequently ignored in practice.* Its most important corollary is that *one* should not think of any single industry or economic activity as more important than any other, and should not therefore concentrate all resources in one particular part of the economy. *Progress must be made on all fronts simultaneously.* In planning for a particular industry or activity, *one* must not put resources into it beyond the point where a transfer of marginal units to some other activity would increase total welfare.'

---

[1] Thus, in par. 216 the report discusses the alternatives of government inducement and government direction of private enterprise. And, in par. 218, it concludes 'the most that governments can hope to do is to start resources moving in the desired directions ; the movement can seldom be controlled precisely in quantity or speed.' In par. 219 we are told that, owing to 'the difficulty of controlling the economy,' it is 'better to concentrate on operating a few strategic controls than to try to control every nook and cranny of the economy.' The paragraph concludes with the statement : '*By controlling a small number of strategic factors, the government can thus determine the pattern of the whole economy.*'

The use of the word ' *one* ' in the above passage is signi-
icant. It does not mean the individual entrepreneur proceed-
ng cautiously and hesitantly (and, indeed, ' experimentally '),
.ccording to the dictates of the market. It means the planner.
Ie, it will be noted, is not to be guided by market indices
ut is to ensure ' that progress must be made on all fronts
imultaneously '. To ensure this, we are informed, it is
1ecessary to have regard ' to the second general principle
vhich economic analysis provides ', and which ' arises from
he fact that large movements of resources within the economy
vill have effects which are disproportionately different from
narginal movements. In consequence, the planner must
.atisfy *himself* not only that further marginal movements
vould serve no useful purpose, *but also that there is nothing
'o be gained* by large *movements of resources*, amounting to a
:onsiderable alteration in the structure of the economy. The
irst of these conditions is often satisfied where the second
s not '. We are not informed by the authors how the planner
vill satisfy himself that ' nothing is to be gained ' by one or
)ther of the movements of resources. However, paragraph
(50 states : 'In under-developed countries major structural
eadjustments are much more needed than they are in
ldvanced countries which have already equipped themselves
vith the basic requirements for economic development. The
narginal principle, therefore, though still valid, is often of
econdary usefulness. *This makes the task of economic calculation
ıll the more difficult.* For, if *one* is working at the margin,
he cost and the productivity of small movements of resources
:an be estimated with fair accuracy, *if only because many such
novements are occurring all the time.* But if *one* is working in
erms of *large structural readjustments*, both cost and produc-
ivity are difficult to measure and *one* is left to rely much more
)n qualitative judgements which can be checked only by the
:vent itself.'

What is significant in this view is the extreme over-
;implification of the problem of structural change. For
;tructural change is a vast process of slowly evolving social
ınd economic re-orientations. It is not at all like the switching
)f factors of production to making one product instead of
ınother ; and it cannot be adequately discussed in terms of

mere ' planning ' decisions. To postulate major structural readjustment is to imply that the goal of change is known ; whereas this is precisely what is not known—unless we are to trust to the intuition of the artist-planner. It is, indeed, unfortunate that the authors speak of the process (e.g., ' *if one is working* in terms of large structural readjustments . . . one is left to rely ' . . . etc., etc.) almost as a sculptor might speak of the inanimate materials which he uses as the medium of expression for his art. But human beings are not a medium of artistic expression ; except for tyrants.

Moreover, to suggest that *rapid* structural changes are what is most required overlooks the fundamental question whether the real problem is not to avoid, as far as possible, all types of ' catastrophic ' action so as to give time for slower —more organic—and less unstable changes ; for the more sudden and the more far-reaching the change the less truly ' experimental ' it is, and the less ' reversible ' it will be. In South Africa, for example, there has been ' major structural change ' of great dimensions. It has been so ' rapid ' and far-reaching for the indigenous inhabitants that it is difficult to see how the masses of people driven by it from their land to the squalid conditions in the new native ' towns ' will find an integrated social life in them in this generation or even the next. Not even an artist can turn his statue back into the rock from which it was rough hewn, if he happens to dislike that which he has made.

It is, indeed, precisely because the authors of the report see economic development primarily as an intellectual or artistic exercise by leaders and governments that they fail to do justice to their examination of existing realities in under-developed countries. Many valuable observations of the report are overshadowed by the mechanistic concepts to which the authors endeavour to relate them. The informative discussion on ' Technology ' (Chapter V) is one example of this ; another is the penetrating observation on the danger that governments, because they ' are directly engaged in public works and are not, in most cases, directly engaged in other productive industry,' will overlook ' the need of their countries for other productive capital ' so that ' capital is

absorbed into public works which would be more pro-
ductively employed in other activities.' (Par. 169.)[1]
In fact, if the authors had not been so imbued with their
own *a priori* concepts of the nature of development they
might have inquired more deeply into the reason for the
tendency which they observed and deplored, that ' the high
standards which some under-developed countries set themselves, sometimes have also the effect of inhibiting the growth
of public works because these works come to be more costly
than the government can afford. For example, in pioneer
settlement of new lands in the nineteenth century, the settlers
often created their own public works for themselves as they
went along. With their own hands, and roughly, they built
their roads, schools, public buildings, water supplies and other
facilities, at a minimum cost. To-day, in some countries,
governments are expected when opening new lands, to cut
down forests, to build good roads, and to provide schools,
water supplies and other community needs, before the first
settlers move in ; and where the government cannot raise the
money required for this heavy initial investment, settlement
is sometimes held up.' (Par. 173). Here is an important clue
—to what in my opinion is the overriding consideration in
the whole question. It is that development depends not on
the abstract national goals of, and the more or less enforced
decisions by, a cadre of planners, but on the piecemeal
adaptation of individuals to goals which emerge but slowly
and become clearer only as those individuals work with the
means at their disposal ; and as they themselves become aware,
in the process of doing, of what can and ought to be done next.

Just as the process of development is not an intellectual
exercise, so it is not merely a process of mass education on
which the authors lean heavily for rapid economic development. Indeed, they tend to make this one of the main con-

[1] The authors add, quite rightly, that the greatest sufferer from preoccupation with
the need for public works is usually small scale farming. ' Much money spent . . . on
improving highways beyond essential standards would be more productive if it were
spent on providing the farmers with better equipment, more good livestock, processing
facilities and such.' (Par. 170.) The authors also point out that ' public works sometimes
absorb too much capital . . . because they are done on too costly a scale. A good
government likes to do properly whatever it may be doing, and especially to leave
behind it structures which are permanent and outstanding. Most under-developed
countries, however, cannot afford the luxury of doing things properly in this sense.'
(Par. 171).

siderations in the choice of the type of education that should be embarked upon. (Pars. 162–166). Accordingly one of the educational priorities is to provide ' *men capable of framing and executing development programs* ' since ' scarcity of such men is one of the major bottlenecks'!

I would be the last to quarrel with the general principle that ' investment in people ' should not suffer at the expense of a too high priority for investment in material resources. However, I am not convinced that these generalizations get us very far unless we are prepared to be far more critical of the fundamental meaning to be attributed to such terms than, from this report at any rate, appears to be the case at present. In my view, a whole people can no more be given rapid economic development by investment in mass education, than it can be given ' democracy ' by ' investment ' in mass political training. For, quite apart from the time all this takes, what is involved is neither just another ready-to-hand goal of action, nor the transfer of a new set of techniques, but the necessarily slow growth of new aptitudes, and of new ways of doing, living, and thinking. We should do everything possible to make the life-giving waters of international culture flow to the uttermost ends of the earth, as the authors are clearly anxious should be the case, but let us beware lest pride in *our* ways of life blind us to the social heritage of others. The problem is not to wipe the slate clean in the under-developed countries, and to write our economic and technical equations on it, but to recognize that different peoples have a different language of social action, and possess, and, indeed, have long exercised, peculiar aptitudes for solving the problems of their own time and place ; aptitudes which must be further developed in the historic setting of their own past to meet the exigencies of the present and the future.

In some sections of the report the authors seem to be aware of these considerations (cf. in particular par. 83 and par. 91). Yet, finally, the reader is left with the impression that either such sections of the report were written by one hand, and the rest of the report by another, or that current preconceptions proved too strong for the authors after all. Nowhere does this lack of historical sensibility come clearer to view than in the important chapter on ' External Capital '.

V. The Need for External Capital

This question is introduced by paragraph 235 as follows : 'To what extent do the under-developed countries need capital from abroad, whether by grant or by loan, if their standards of living are to rise appreciably? This is clearly a very difficult question to answer. It involves making very hazardous guesses as to their present national incomes, their rates of population increase, and the cost and productivity of different types of investment. . . . In the circumstances, we have debated at some length whether it would serve any useful purpose to suggest any figures in this sphere, and whether we should not merely leave the matter by saying that these countries will progress faster if they get more capital, and more slowly if they get less.' I think it was a pity that the authors decided after all to embark upon a series of most hazardous estimates. These estimates are not only, in my opinion, statistically unwarranted, but I believe that they completely fail to indicate ' the magnitude of what is involved,' as the authors thought they would, because the assumptions as to what is involved are in themselves either fallacious or unsupported by sufficient evidence. In any case the statistical assumptions are capable of so many variations and inter-pretations that almost any other ' order of magnitude ' could have been obtained by even slightly different assumptions. The calculations, though executed with care, are in my opinion not meaningful in theory, nor practical as the basis of policy.

Table 2 on page 76 ' shows the capital required by the under-developed countries of the world for two purposes—to increase the national income by transferring population out of agriculture[1] into non-farm occupations, and to increase agricultural yields.' (Par. 236). The authors in paragraph 238 assume ' an annual transfer out of agriculture of 1 per cent of the total working population into employment other than in agriculture.' They state : ' In one sense, this may

---

[1] I have already criticized some of the basic concepts involved here. No further evidence is submitted by the authors for their contention that industrialization is ' everywhere of the highest priority, whether because of the superior productivity of industry, or because the improvement of agricultural techniques will reduce the need for labour in agriculture, or because the land is already overcrowded.' (Par. 237).

H

seem rather a high rate of transfer, since in most countries it *would* increase industrial output by more than 10 per cent per annum. On the other hand, at present rates of population growth *it would still not be enough* in most areas to reduce the *absolute number* of persons engaged in agriculture. Neither is a 10 per cent increase in industrial production in any way unusual for countries which are just beginning their industrial development.' No evidence is presented for these assumptions. Statistically speaking they are anybody's guess. But the next guess, in paragraph 239, raises much more than statistical issues. The authors take the sum of $2,500 as the amount of capital ' required for *each person* absorbed into non-agricultural employment.' This, they say, is ' an average which takes into account the low amounts required by those who go into light industries, and the very high amounts required in heavy industries and in public utilities. It also includes expenditure on industrial research and on training.'

' This,' continues the report, ' gives us the figure . . . of $15,270 million *a year* for the under-developed world as a whole, of which 70 per cent is required for Asia.' The authors then proceed : ' *It* should be noted that the cost of industrialization, as a ratio of the national income, varies inversely with national income per capita.' The reason for this statement, namely that ' Industrialization requires a larger part of the national income in poor countries than it does in rich countries because as *between countries, the cost of industrial capital per worker does not vary very much,*' shows, in my opinion, that the authors have failed to grasp that the basic problem of development in under-developed countries consists precisely in the fact that it is essential to utilize more adequately and fully the *labour* resources as they now are in those countries, so as gradually to build up new forms of capital suited to the specific environment, resources, and aptitudes of the people themselves. The way to accumulate capital in these countries is in general (if one must speak in general terms, which I do with misgiving on this question) to make the best use of that factor which is most abundant, i.e., labour—not to displace it by capital, which is relatively scarce, and has to be imported at considerable cost. It is wrong to imply, as the authors do, that there has to be a *sudden, rapid,* and almost *revolutionary* shift to an entirely new structure of production in under-developed countries ; to postulate a capital intensity in them akin to that which is found in the more advanced countries is unwarranted. Moreover, such revolutionary economic change may be economically and socially dangerous. It is apt to lead to an unnecessary degree of both economic and social disintegration. It may dissociate people from their established social patterns of living too rapidly, and so reduce them to the status of uprooted wage earners without the security previously provided by their social system. And it may establish a capital structure and types of activity, which the economy cannot continue to support when the flow of investment or aid from abroad ceases.

The real reason for the erroneous approach of the authors is, I believe, that they think of capital and employment in abstract terms. Thus although they realize that high capital intensity requires a different and very specialist type of labour (in terms of skill, reliability, economic adaptability, and acquaintance with the machine, etc.) they do not appear to appreciate fully how very long it takes to develop that 'efficiency', and the general industrial ethos which it presupposes. Mere ' training ' is quite unable to create the human ' external economies ' of an industrial society, nor is it possible to ' wait ' for training to remould society. Society in the last resort remoulds itself by the process of action. What is most required, therefore, is both a simpler and a more human approach which, in the first instance, looks at the problems of the under-developed countries as their peoples themselves experience them, and as they themselves can best contribute to the solution of them. Capital, in accounting terms, always appears to be a matter of investment, saving, and accumulation in banks and similar institutions—on which the report dilates at length. Capital accumulation in the under-developed world, however, with the hand-to-mouth struggle of its peoples, is a far less abstract matter. For what is really involved is the evolution of a different art of living and working. In all the multitudinous aspects of their daily life the peoples of the under-developed world require to perfect new attitudes and aptitudes : be they in maintaining the fertility of the land, or in educating their children ; or be they in hygiene, nutrition, and general habits of consumption and production.

It is not an accident that men and women born and bred in a naturally ' poor ' country—Scotland—not only developed it, but through the thrifty habits and aptitudes acquired at home prospered in large numbers abroad, and indeed brought, by their thrift and enterprise, prosperity to those areas through-out the world to which many of them migrated. As Alfred Marshall saw so well, economic development is, in the last resort, largely determined by, and in turn determines, the growth of a particular type of ' character ' or behaviour. Similarly, that incorruptibility in administration, on the need for which the report lays such stress, will not result from mere commands or exhortations. All such changes are necessarily slow, and cannot be greatly influenced by the rapid injection of capital from abroad. In fact, of course, the belief in the miracles to be wrought by ' capital investment ' *per se* is an illusion. In particular, it overlooks the fact that the essence of capital itself is that it wears out rapidly unless continually renewed, replaced, or maintained. The ' poorer ' a country in skilled labour and in national resources, the less capital it is likely to have, *and the less it can afford to have*, until the whole social and economic complex of its activities has gradually evolved patterns of economic behaviour suited to its use, reproduction, and further accumulation.

But let me return to the main calculations of the report. After assuming that the under-developed countries should spend ' 1 per cent of their national incomes on agricultural extension services and research ; and that a further 3 per cent per annum should be invested in agricultural capital on and off the farms ' the authors arrive, finally, at the total figure of about $19 billion *per year* as the capital required. In regard thereto they state (par. 241) ' If anyone thinks this large, he should compare it with net investment in the United States of America, which now runs at between $25 and $30 billion a year for a population one-tenth the size of that which we are considering, and for an economy that is already highly developed.' They add, that, for the under-developed countries, ' the total capital requirement, including the capital required for social overheads, greatly exceeds $19 billion.' Just exactly what light, if any, total net investment in the United States throws on the theoretical and practical problems of the entirely different economies of the under-developed countries I find it difficult to understand.

However, the authors are not at the end of their statistical resources, for, in paragraph, 242, they now endeavour to answer the question : ' If the investment of $19 billion were made in industry and agriculture, by how much per annum would production increase? ' They reply : ' We have assumed an annual shift of 1 per cent of the total working population into industry. This should *originate* national income to the extent of about 2 per cent, after allowing for capital charges. In countries which have surplus labour in agriculture, this would be equivalent to an annual net increase in the national income of 2 per cent. But, in other countries, the net increase is equal only to the difference between the productivity of labour in industry and the productivity of labour in agriculture, from which it has been withdrawn. We may assume that, *over the under-developed world as a whole*, the shift might increase the national income by $1\frac{1}{2}$ per cent per annum.'

Space forbids a detailed examination of the rest of the calculations, including estimates of improvements in agricultural yields. They are further refined to take account of population growth, and to show, not only how national incomes will increase, but also how the standard of living in these countries will be affected after population growth has absorbed some of the increased incomes.

There are, however, certain theoretical considerations arising out of the above calculation which warrant a brief reference. What possible basis exists for the categorical statement that the $19 billion dollars investment ' should *originate* national income to the extent of 2 per cent ' or indeed any other percentage? Capital investment *per se* does not originate anything other than the capital expenditure itself. It is people, who, if they possess the disposition, aptitudes, experience and knowledge, and if they find suitable environmental opportunities, alone can *originate* anything at all. Whether investment will produce net income, or, indeed, any income, or whether it will simply rust, like some of the railway lines built prematurely at great capital cost in Africa, depends not only on the correct investment of the capital in the right directions, but even more on the continuous successful management and handling of it in a suitable socio-economic environment. Only then will that true surplus be achieved from which alone income can be obtained. The whole process is such an uncertain one, that, in view of the past history of investment, and of foreign investment in particular, it is astonishing to find the implication that capital investment automatically yields income, and to be told, moreover, that the yield of industrial investment can be expected ' to grow cumulatively.' (Par. 244).

In paragraph 246 the authors next endeavour to show that domestic saving in the year 1949 fell short of ' what our estimates require ' (i.e., $19 billion) by $14 billion ; and, after further assumptions, they express the belief ' that a 2 per cent increase in the per capita national incomes cannot be brought about without an annual capital import well in excess of $10 billion.' In paragraph 248 they state categorically : ' These amounts are large, but they are not beyond the capacity of the developed countries to provide. The national incomes of the countries of Western Europe, Australasia, the United States, and Canada aggregate about $350 billion a year. If they were to transfer 2 per cent of this amount annually to the under-developed countries, it would be equal to $7 billion a year. Neither would this be a very high target. In 1905–1913, the United Kingdom exported capital to the extent of an annual average of £143 million, which was 7 per cent of her annual national income. And, similarly, loans and grants from the United States of America have been running at over 3 per cent of her national income in the past five years '. From a theoretical point of view I believe the comparison with what occurred in the United Kingdom in 1905–1913 is not meaningful. These statistics are historical data, and refer wholly to the past. They refer to a particular conjuncture of events, to a period, indeed, when world economic relations were very different. Moreover, the export of British capital was part and parcel of the creation of a larger economic and trading area in which there was an unprecedented mobility not only of goods but of

people, and in which capital investment was on the whole
assured of treatment by governments suited to its further
accumulation. It is actually of interest, in this connexion,
that many historians and economists have argued (whether
rightly or wrongly is not a matter of importance here) that the
export of capital from Britain was excessive ; they allege that
the standard of life of the British people was lowered thereby.
I mention the matter merely to show that it is insufficient
to argue from such past events that, for example (par. 263),
since ' The countries of Western Europe have now recovered
from the dislocation of the war . . . it is *proper* that they, as
well as Canada, and other *relatively* wealthy countries, should
also play their part in making capital available to the under-
developed world '. Nor is the comparison with the rate at
which the United States has made loans and grants in recent
years much more helpful—since these were on the whole
made to the so-called ' advanced ' countries of Europe to
assist them on account of the post-war situation in which they
found themselves. In any case what is thought to be ' proper '
will in the last resort come to be decided not on the basis of
vague generalizations but in accordance with the results—
in terms of mutual benefits—which are expected to be achieved,
and which are indeed achieved, in developing the under-
developed countries.

VI. Private Investment, Government Lending, and Intergovernmental Grants

Following upon these calculations the authors consider in
turn investment, government lending, and intergovernmental
grants-in-aid, as means to provide the large sums of capital
which they have found are required by the under-developed
countries.

The few pages devoted to private investment indicate
that the authors do not take a very optimistic view of the
future course of private investment. This is natural in view
of the well-known existing obstacles : extreme autarchic and
nationalistic policies, political uncertainties, and general
fiscal and economic discrimination against private investment.
It is, however, a pity that the authors did not come out more

strongly against existing discriminations by exposing their theoretical and practical incompatibility with their own plans for development. The reason for this failure is, I believe, that they did not succeed in freeing themselves from their own autarchic, and largely national, approach to the whole problem. As an example, the following statement is significant (par. 255): 'Some under-developed countries do not look very favourably upon this kind of investment. They fear foreign control of important sectors of their economy. Or they consider that the cost of foreign private capital is too high. For example, the average rate of return on United States foreign investments in 1948 was about 17 per cent, compared with about 14 per cent on United States domestic investments. Many under-developed countries *feel* that this is too high a price to pay for capital.' This is hardly a very helpful way of dealing with this issue ; it is not meaningful to endeavour to arrive at a suitable 'price' for capital on the basis of *average* returns. The 'return on investments' (it is not defined as net or gross) is not a 'price' at all. It depends, in the last resort, on the unforeseeable results of the investment and is a residual item (a quasi-rent). For some types of investment a return of 17 per cent may actually be low, if much time has elapsed before the investment begins to show a return at all ; and if the risk of loss is great. In any case, the difference between the figures quoted for the average return on foreign investments and domestic investments is not necessarily unduly high, taking the greater risks of the foreign investments into account, and assuming, for the moment, that such averages are meaningful. The authors, however, do not seem to realize the full implication of their argument. If under-developed countries cannot show as high a return, or hold out a prospect therefor, as is obtainable elsewhere, then their argument implies that investments which yield a larger surplus (and therefore opportunities for the more rapid accumulation of capital) should be held up in order to conduct development where the returns and opportunities are much smaller. If this is, indeed, their argument it would have been interesting to have been informed how far they think the process of damping down investment in the more suitable regions should be carried.

Another example of the nationalistic attitude of the authors is provided in paragraph 258. We are told that : ' However well-intentioned the government of an under-developed country may be, it cannot absolutely guarantee that foreign investors will be permitted to remit their profits home in foreign currency, or to retire their investments, because it has not the power to ensure that the necessary foreign exchange will always be available.' However, in paragraph 261, we read ' the flow of private investment is partly a function of the amount which the governments of the under-developed countries spend on improving basic facilities, and on health and education. The bigger the public investment is, the bigger *will* be the private investment '. I fear that the history of certain South American, and Southern and Eastern European countries does not support this contention. Liberal government expenditure in those areas was frequently a signal to the private investor to curtail his commitments before those countries could no longer meet their obligations abroad. The fact is, that it always rests with the government to pursue economic or uneconomic fiscal and monetary policies ; and if it pursues the latter it will, of course, no longer be able to guarantee that the foreign investors will be permitted to remit their profits home in foreign currency ; indeed the country will then probably not even have enough foreign currency for essential imports. The real issue has nothing to do with the alleged *good intentions* of governments but is a question of good government itself—i.e., of the rule of law, so that contractual obligations will be safeguarded, and the rights of foreigners will not be considered merely as residual items in autarchic juggling with the balance of payments.

Although the authors stated that the figures arrived at in their main calculations should not ' be taken exactly ', but only as an ' order of magnitude ', the section on government lending apparently makes considerable use of these estimates. It roundly, and, I believe, unfairly, criticizes the International Bank for Reconstruction and Development (par. 264) and, finally, exhorts it ' to do everything that lies in its power to *break down the obstacles to sound investment* in the under-developed countries. The Bank should set itself to reach, within five years, some such target as an annual rate *of lending of not* *less than $1 billion a year to the under-developed countries. If it shows no sign of approaching this target, the whole question of the proper international organization for the provision of adequate amounts of loan capital to the under-developed countries should be reviewed by the United Nations.'* (Par. 268). Since they are either inherent in the social and economic structure of the countries requiring capital, or are (unfortunately very frequently) the direct result of autarchic economic and fiscal policies, and even of various misguided planning schemes, it is not surprising that the report does not attempt to indicate how the International Bank should proceed to *break down* these obstacles. The authors have, however, no hesitation at all in asserting that (par. 267) : 'A further obstacle to greater lending by the bank is the unpreparedness of some governments. There is, to begin with, the fact that some governments have not an *adequate will* to develop, or where the will is present, have not always an adequate conception of what is involved. The part of the world most *afflicted* by this is probably the Continent of Africa, *some of whose governments are too proud to borrow* for colonial development, and others of which lack understanding of the magnitude of their task, or even believe *rapid* economic development is not in their interest or in the interest of the African people. Hardly any of the powers now governing Africa can afford to spare for domestic development the vast sums needed for developing that Continent (*well over $1 billion annually*) and there is not much hope of rapid progress unless they seek capital in the international market.'

If all this had any relation to realities it would be difficult to see what exactly the Bank for International Development should do to mould the will of governments (and particularly ' proud ones ') to the authors' liking, and to make the will and the aptitudes of the peoples of the African continent more amenable to its concepts of progress. However, as one who has spent the greater part of his life as an economist in dealing with the investment problems of Africa, and indeed in trying to contribute to the greater economic and political liberty of its inhabitants, I can say that a statement of this kind is so unrelated to the basic problems of the continent and its peoples as to be quite irrelevant. Some of the persons involved in recent attempts by the British Government to hasten development through the expenditure of very large sums of capital per annum in the heart of Africa, might, however, be able to enlighten the authors of this report about the reasons why their figure of $1 billion *annually* of new capital investment in that continent is, to say the least, at present somewhat wide of the mark.

The final section of this chapter of the report makes the suggestion that an International Development Authority should be established to decide upon and administer the distribution of grants-in-aid for various purposes, and to verify their utilization. The proposal includes further recommendations that the authority should co-operate with under-developed countries in the preparation and co-ordination of plans of economic development ; should help in implementing development plans especially in the procurement of scarce resources ; should make periodic reports regarding the preparation and progress of plans of development ; should provide for continuous study of the problems of economic development of under-developed countries; and should make recommendation to the Economic and Social Council in regard to any action that may be required concerning these problems. It suggests that the following purposes should be considered eligible for grants, and that other purposes, which are more capable of being self-supporting, should be financed by borrowing : (*a*) research and education, (*b*) public health programmes, (*c*) subsidization of medium and short-term farm credit, (*d*) improvement of rural public works, etc.

The distinction between purposes which should be financed by grants-in-aid and those which should be financed by borrowing or the investment of equity capital is important. The principle of finance through grants-in-aid is one which has a long history in colonial development. There is every reason to make use of this device provided that there are proper sanctions for the economical use of the grants so provided. The question at issue is not merely one of *verifying* expenditures ; it goes much deeper than that. Such grants-in-aid should carry with them definite obligations by the countries receiving them to co-operate in all those directions necessary for the integration of their countries into the free world economy. In saying this I do not have in mind the point which the authors raise in paragraph 278, where they state : ' some countries are ruled by corrupt or reactionary cliques whose regime might be overthrown by the people if there were no foreign aid, and who may be settled in their rule because foreign grants have become available. Members of the United Nations will not wish to have had any hand in fastening such governments on peoples. They might therefore wish to lay down certain minimum conditions before an under-developed country was admitted to the list of those eligible to receive grants. This is a most controversial matter, on which we do not make any recommendation.' This was a very wise decision. It would be more than invidious for the United Nations to have to consider problems of technical assistance as part of a political judgment concerned with whether or not *particular* governments are corrupt or reactionary. What I have in mind, in referring to sanctions, is something much more objective : namely, the observance of agreed rules to ensure that *governments* which receive technical or financial aid from an international authority, shall adhere to agreements intended to promote international economic intercourse, and shall refrain from pursuing autarchic and discriminating policies which undermine the movement of factors of production, and of men and women across national frontiers for productive purposes.

Whether an International Development Authority is necessary in order to implement existing methods of international technical assistance is to my mind an open question. Its answer, I believe, will largely depend on whether or not it is possible for the United Nations to ensure that the decisions of the proposed Authority will really be objective, and will take into account the interests of both those who grant and those who receive aid.

VII. Concluding Observations

This brings me to some concluding observations on the whole report. There is no escape from the real issue which, I fear, the authors have failed to face. It is that the capital

esources of the world are not abundant but scarce ; that
heir premature or wasteful application anywhere is harmful
o the peoples of the world as a whole ; that as capital is so
carce the main problem is how to produce more of it in the
places where it can be most readily and easily produced ; that
his is a task which demands the creation of a suitable code of
nternational conduct under which both borrowers and
enders will be forced to act responsibly—both in investing
capital, and in the use of capital so invested.

I cannot support the belief that international capital
nvestment can be considered mainly as a national political
contest for the distribution of vast sums (some of which
may even have to be raised by means of inflationary finance,
or fiscal measures inimical to enterprise, in the lending
countries) to be spent in accordance with principles which
do not necessarily have any relation to the comparative
productivity of the capital in the different regions to which it
s allocated.

It is one of the greatest defects of this report that it fails
to disclose the criteria which are to be used in deciding which
countries are to receive (and in what proportions) the large
sums it proposes should be spent every year. It fails to give
reasons why any one country should get capital rather than
any other. Is the allocation to be, let us say, on the basis of
the relative populations of the under-developed areas? What
would then be left for any country whose population is not
counted in hundreds of millions? Alternatively is it intended
that the allocation be made on the basis of arbitrary per capita
income calculations—which, unfortunately, have little relation
to the real economic situation in different countries? Should
the capital be given to those who husband it ; who develop
political habits of good government ; who support the free
mobility of goods, and the immigration of skill and labour ;
who defer to the rule of law ; and who encourage the confidence of foreign investors in the integrity of their governments ; or is it to be allocated to those whose political habits
and institutions cannot be relied upon for co-operant world
economic intercourse, and who have not attracted, and do not
make an effort to attract, either the capital or those who can
manage its investment?

Perhaps it is wrong to raise such questions. My excuse for raising them is that the people of the under-developed territories of the world yearn for new hope and new opportunity To make hope depend merely on the illusion of rapid change which it is supposed to be in the *power* of the few to bring about for the benefit of the many, is to invite a vast disillusion ment. This may well destroy the opportunities which still exist for action to revive the security of both public and private enterprise within, and, especially, *across* national frontiers ; and for the creation of a really *independent* international civil service to assist those under-developed countries *and peoples* that are prepared to make proper and objective use of such assistance.

I regretfully conclude that this report exhibits a tendency in the United Nations to promote inquiries into important economic matters in unduly general terms. It is not fair to distinguished experts to invite them to answer questions so vaguely formulated, and so ill-defined, as were the terms of reference of this one.

ESSAY VI

WHITHER SOUTH AFRICA?

I. Introduction

THE title of this essay may mislead some of my readers to expect me to indulge in prophecy. That is not the function of the economist, who, indeed, is popularly held to be more successful in explaining the inevitability of an event after it has occurred, than in forecasting its happening. The title I have chosen is based on the old proverb ' Know who you are, where you are from, and where you are going '.

It is my object to draw attention to some of the fundamental economic forces which have fashioned modern South Africa, to certain beliefs and institutions within the framework of which these forces have operated, and to certain decisions which confront the people of South Africa in relation to the organization of their economic activities in the future.

The history of South Africa might well be written around a series of miracles, if we can so designate those remarkable occurrences which time and again have confounded current prognostications. It is an astonishing story.

For centuries the sub-continent repelled newcomers to its shores owing to its poverty-ridden aspect, its vast distances, its mountain ranges and lack of navigable rivers (which barred entry into the interior), its large areas of irregular rainfall and poor soils, its tropical diseases and agricultural pests, and its primitive indigenous peoples.

Until the last quarter of the nineteenth century the modern history of South Africa can be characterized as a struggle between the feudal eighteenth century society of the European immigrant population, which penetrated from the South, and the pastoral pagan Bantu societies which, migrating from the North, were eventually overcome by the European colonists.

Who could have forecast a hundred years ago when this era was drawing to a dramatic close that the descendants of these diverse peoples, the one largely isolated from the European civilization which it had left, the other meeting a civilization such as it had never known, would, within a hundred years, build in this land of apparent poverty an economy equipped with every modern productive device? Indeed, that economy became strong enough to support the Union in two world wars to defend the civilization of its European ancestors, and to emerge stronger from the conflict on both occasions.

II. The Impact of World Economy

The Industrial Revolution, and the World Economy, burst upon South Africa with the discovery of diamonds and, subsequently, of gold. These unforeseen events encouraged also the final stage of exploration of the African Continent as a whole. With these mineral discoveries there began, not only a new political, but also a new economic era—both for the patriarchal society of the white and for the tribal organization of the black man. Very few prophecies have been so literally fulfilled as that of the then Colonial Secretary when, one day in 1867, he laid upon the table of the Cape House of Assembly one of the earliest diamonds discovered in South Africa, and said, ' Gentlemen, this is the rock on which the future success of South Africa will be built '.

Diamond production proved the most effective means for obtaining surplus wealth with which to buy from abroad the capital instruments which South Africa so sorely required to open up its vast territories, and to span them with modern means of communication. Moreover, it altered the manner in which Europe regarded the Cape Colony : establishing it in the eyes of the old world as a land of new possibilities in its own right, instead of a somewhat troublesome half-way house to India. I have shown elsewhere[1] how the diamond pioneers, by establishing the financial nexus between Europe and Kimberley, enabled the South African colonies to take full advantage of the second miraculous occurrence—the discovery of gold on the Witwatersrand in 1886 ; this led

[1] S. Herbert Frankel : *Capital Investment in Africa. Its Course and Effects.* Oxford University Press, 1938.

to a renewed wave of migration of capital and men from overseas to the economically barren interior.

Very few prophetic remarks as to the future role which gold-mining would play in the history of the country marked the opening of the richest goldfields in the world. Indeed, it is significant for an understanding, not only of the past, but of the present, that ever since the discovery of gold on the Witwatersrand, both South African and overseas experts were often more concerned with warnings as to the not far distant decline of the industry, than with its potentialities. It is possible that their fears resulted from the experience of the relatively short-lived gold-mining fields, of smaller extent, in California and Australia. Whatever the reason, it is probably due to this pessimism that economic policy in South Africa towards mining, taxation, and labour questions has been unnecessarily affected by what might be called ' the mining-camp mentality ' : which is more concerned with what might happen when the mining camp will be deserted than with the conditions which have to be fulfilled in order that it should continue.

Gold has played the same part, relatively speaking, in the emergence of South Africa as an economic power, as coal did in Great Britain. It did not, it is true, feed the furnaces of its export industries. Gold itself was the export with which South Africa bought from abroad the capital and consumer goods which have established modern standards of life for its inhabitants. Gold-mining continues to occupy this pre-eminent, and so far irreplaceable position in the South African economy.

With the end of the Boer War came the third wave of migration of men and capital. This was followed by a radical alteration in the technique of mining and metallurgy, which led to the opening of the deep-level gold mines, and the great boom in 1911. There followed the First World War, the rise in costs of mining, and the steady decline, with minor cyclical interruptions, until 1932. Thereafter, the series of changes which raised the world price of gold encouraged those boom conditions which, with very minor setbacks, lasted until the war, were fanned by the war economy, and have gained a new lease of life through the discovery of the

I

remarkable new goldfields of the Orange Free State, and the large capital investments from abroad which they have stimulated.[1]

Just as in the case of the First World War, so the Second World War gave a great impetus to the growth of manufacturing industry. Much of this expansion is again likely to prove permanent. Moreover, throughout this period of the modern economic history of the Union, agricultural production has drawn heavily on the capital resources made directly and indirectly available from mining revenues, and has expanded in response to both export and growing home markets.

In the face of this repeated beckoning of the finger of fate, who would dare to be a pessimist in regard to the natural resources of South Africa? What peoples have had greater opportunities showered upon them to assist them in their struggle with a new, and in many other respects so difficult an environment? For, in addition to gold and diamonds, and platinum, exploration has disclosed important base mineral resources, in particular, valuable low-cost coal and iron deposits, which have enabled the creation of an iron and steel industry and could, given those changes to which I shall refer later, lead to a wide complex of modern chemical and engineering industries based thereon.

Moreover, although it is usual to speak popularly of South Africa as a poor agricultural country, in fact it contains large areas suitable to specialized agricultural and pastoral production for export, and also other regions well able to produce by modern methods all of the food supplies of a much greater population than that which now inhabits the country. I doubt if any scientific observer, however pessimistic he might be inclined to be, would seriously argue that the Union has yet dealt as effectively as it could with its agricultural possibilities—or has faced up to the changes in customary methods which modern scientific agriculture demands.

---

[1] And now, in 1952, the production of uranium, just begun, promises to yield within a few years an export income second in amount only to gold itself.

III. Growth of the National Income

This cursory glance at the natural resources of the country can usefully be supplemented by a brief account of noteworthy changes in the National Income. If we take the periods 1911–12 to 1919–20 (Period 1) and 1922–23 to 1928–29 (Period 2), and 1932–33 to 1938–39 (Period 3), each of which, broadly speaking, commences a year after a depression or recession reached its lowest point (and each of which ends with the peak year of the subsequent boom), we get three comparable periods in the history of the Union which are of great interest. We find that the National Income at constant prices per head of the gainfully occupied population increased at an average annual rate of 1.4 per cent in the first period, 2.5 per cent in the second, and 5.3 per cent in the third period. It will be noted that the rate of growth in the third period was more than double the corresponding rate of increase in the second period, and that the rate of growth in the second period had already been nearly double that which was achieved in the first. Indeed, the rate of expansion of the National Income in South Africa during the period of recovery after the 1932 depression has been one of the most rapid in the world.[1]

The net National Income[2] produced (at current prices) was in 1911–12 about £131 millions. At the outbreak of the war it had reached nearly £395 millions (for the year 1938–39). Allowing for changes in the value of money, and for the increase in the occupied population, it is found that between 1911–12 and 1938–39 the real income per head of the total occupied population increased from £48.4 in 1911–12 to £77.3 in 1938–39, an increase of 59.7 per cent. During the war the National Income at constant prices continued to increase. At about £544 millions for the year 1945–46, it was some 33 per cent greater than before the war.

[1] Cf. S. Herbert Frankel (assisted by H. Herzfeld) 'An Analysis of the Growth of the National Income of the Union in the Period of Prosperity before the War,' *South African Journal of Economics*, June, 1944, vol. 12, No. 2, and ' Consumption, Investment and War Expenditure in Relation to the National Income ', *South African Journal of Economics*, September 1946, vol. 14, No. 3.

[2] Figures for Transactions with the ' Rest of the World ' are not available until 1941–42, so prior to that date the ' National Income ' statistics are more accurately described as ' Geographical Income '.

For 1950–51 the net National Income was £1,114 millions, as compared with £690 millions of 1946–47, an increase of 62 per cent. According to the new Real Income Index now published by the South African Bureau of Census and Statistics (see p. 175, *South African Journal of Economics*, Vol. 20, No. 2, 1952), it appears that the corresponding real National Income, calculated by deflating the expenditure, at market prices, by the retail prices index, increased by about 30%.[1]

I cannot deal in detail here with these great changes, and I must confine myself to a few significant aspects thereof.

IV. Dependence on International Trade

First, I should like to draw attention to the fact that the Union is still greatly dependent on international trade, and obtains a large comparative advantage therefrom. One can say that the present equipment of South Africa in material capital, and in the skill of its inhabitants, is of a kind which, directly or indirectly, is still largely based on a system of production for export. Before the war about three persons out of eight in the working population were engaged either in the production or the transportation or the distribution of primary products for export, but since then the proportion has clearly declined, although figures to indicate the exact extent of the decline are not available. Thus, a rise or fall in employment in the export industries results in a more than proportionate rise or fall in employment in that part of the economy which produces goods and services for the home market. In other words, specialization enables the Union to obtain a greater real National Income by exchanging its exports for imported commodities, which latter the country cannot produce in the same quantities and/or qualities, or at the same cost as it imports them. It is noteworthy that of the total value of exports (excluding re-exports) in the period 1932–33 to 1938–39, the exports of minerals accounted for over 76 per cent (of these mineral exports over 71 per cent were gold exports), whereas the average annual value of

---

[1] I am not able to express these figures on a strictly comparable basis for all years since 1938–39, because since the South African Bureau of Census and Statistics took over my calculations of the National Income in 1946 changes and improvements in the calculations have been made by it.

agricultural exports only accounted for about 20 per cent. This decline in the relative importance of agricultural exports, which had been almost continuous, up to the outbreak of the war, has in recent years been arrested. The value of agricultural exports in 1949 was 29 per cent of all exports ; mineral exports were 60 per cent while exports of gold now formed 73 per cent of the mineral exports.

The extent of the expansion of manufacturing industry can be judged from a number of viewpoints. In the first place there has been a steady increase in the net product of secondary industry. In 1926–27 this amounted to £33 millions ; by 1938–39 it had reached nearly £70 millions ; at the end of the war (1945–46) it was £140 millions ; and for 1950–51 it was £269 millions. This expansion has naturally been reflected in the number of workers employed. From 124,000 in 1916–17 the number rose to 203,000 in 1926–27, to 352,000 in 1938–39, to 489,000 at the end of the war (1945), and to 668,000 in 1948–49. The significance of these numbers can be more readily grasped when contrasted with those employed elsewhere. In 1926–27 the largest industry was mining with 354,000 employees of all races, and at that time manufacturing absorbed only 203,000. Yet by 1948–49 manufacturing employees had increased threefold to 668,000, whereas mining employees had risen by little more than a third to 485,000. Indeed in 1948–49 there were more people employed in manufacturing alone than in 1926–27 in manufacturing, on the railways and harbours, and in mining combined, when the total labour employed in all these came to 651,000.

Nevertheless, notwithstanding the expansion in manufacturing industry, the value of exports produced by it remained very small until after the last war. The average annual value of manufactured exports was only just over £2,500,000 for the period 1932–33 to 1938–39, equivalent to only 2.5 per cent of the Union's total exports. However by 1949 the value of manufactured exports had reached £26.3 million equivalent to 10 per cent of all exports from the Union. It is important to note that 50 per cent of all raw materials used in manufacturing industry before the war were imported ; and that notwithstanding the expansion of manufacturing exports, in 1948–49 the corresponding ratio was still 46 per cent. At the same time the cost of imported raw materials used rose from £49 millions before the war (1938-39) to £362 millions in 1948-49. Manufacturing industry itself is thus not yet able to supply more than a small proportion of the exchange resources which it requires for its productive activities and their expansion. These exchange resources have to be obtained from the sale of the Union's other exports.

The Union's experience in this connexion has more than local significance. It throws into sharp relief the problems of industrialization in other African territories and, indeed, in other backward areas of the world. It is sometimes hastily assumed that more effective employment in such territories can be provided by increased self-sufficiency and by the diversion of labour resources from industries producing for export to industries producing for the home market—in particular to secondary industries. The experience of the Union shows the fallacy of this belief and indicates the importance of maintaining exports, either in the form of additional manufactured products, or in the form of raw materials. If an economy has attained to certain income standards on the basis of appreciable advantages from international trade, then if these advantages should for any reason be reduced in the future, the National Income per head will fall, unless the structure of the economy can be so modified as to make good the loss of the real income from this source.

V. THE TRANSFORMATION OF SUBSISTENCE ECONOMY

The second point to which I would invite your attention is that, notwithstanding the fortunate opportunities and developments to which I have referred, the overall picture which the Union's economy presents is still one of great poverty for the mass of its inhabitants. That poverty is difficult to express in statistical terms[1] ; it has, however, been the main aspect of its economic life to which various private observers and official commissions have drawn attention. What is most significant is that, while European

[1] Some of the theoretical difficulties have been discussed in Essay No. III in this volume.

ncome levels, taken separately, now reflect both an absolute
evel, and a range in the various income categories, not very
different from those in Australia, or even Canada, non-
European incomes are very much lower than European
ncomes.

This situation can be partly illustrated from the statistics
of incomes earned in various employments. In 1926–27
here were 122,000 non-Europeans in manufacturing industry
earning a total of £6.2 millions or £50 per capita. Europeans
numbered 81,000 and earned £17.8 millions or £219 per
capita. In railways in 1927 there were 40,000 non-European
employees with total wages of £1.9 millions (£47 per capita),
and 54,000 Europeans receiving £13.1 millions (£242 per
capita). That is to say that European wages per head were
some four times as high as non-European wages. In mining
the gap between the earnings of the two groups was even
greater. In 1928 there were 323,000 non-Europeans in that
industry with total wages of £9.1 millions (£28 per capita),
and 38,000 Europeans receiving £10.8 millions (£278 per
capita), i.e. a wage nearly ten times that of the non-European.
A quarter of a century later this basic relationship has not
changed. In manufacturing, European wages per head in
1948–49 were £473, i.e. still some four times that of the non-
European figure of £128 ; in Railways (including Harbours)
Europeans earned in 1949–50 £512 per head, and non-
Europeans £137 ; in mining, the 1950 figures show the
amount per head earned by Europeans to be £710 and non-
Europeans £51, a ratio of 14 to 1.[1]

Of even greater significance is the contrast between the
earnings of non-Europeans in the towns and the subsistence
' incomes ' in the native areas. These are not statistically
comparable—they represent two different ' economic worlds '.
Rough calculations made in 1936 indicated an average
' income ' of only some £3 per head per occupied person.
It is probable that this figure had risen to about £6 or £8 by
1950.

While a large part of the non-European peoples in the
Union is still confined to subsistence production, yielding

[1] This excludes the provision, generally made by mining companies for their non-
European employees of free quarters and food.

an extremely low standard of life comparable to that which continues to dominate the economy of most of Africa, it is probably true to say that the most characteristic feature of the Union's economic history during the last fifty years has been the tempo with which its indigenous peoples have been swept into the modern economy.

The economic structure of capitalist economy in South Africa is thus one of industrial caste. Whereas in non-caste societies men are promoted on the ladder of achievement, with appropriate allowances for minor non-economic factors, in South Africa the non-economic factors predominate : non-European workers can climb a few rungs of the economic ladder only to find the next section barred to their advance. Indeed, for the great mass of non-Europeans there is only one section of the ladder—that of unskilled labour, and that section has very few rungs of promotion.

VI. The ' Multi-Racial Team System '

For all practical purposes the laws, customs and institutions of the Union have the effect of bringing about a situation in which productive power is circumscribed by race. Economic activity is organized on the basis of utilizing workers in what can perhaps be described as a ' multi-racial team system '. Over large sections of economic enterprise those responsible can increase or decrease the size of the team, but they cannot easily vary its proportionate racial composition, or alter the scale of remuneration or the nature of the tasks allotted to the different races of which the team is composed.

This peculiar system must not be regarded as absolutely rigid. As so frequently happens reality has played many tricks on those who cling to outworn conceptions of it. There are already considerable breaches in the system. Thus, while in 1926–27 there were 10,600 European and 7,800 non-European women in all factories, by the end of the war in 1944–45 the numbers had risen to 35,000 and 24,000 respectively and since then there has been a still further increase to 41,000 European women employees and 33,500 non-European women employees in 1948–49. Moreover, many semi-skilled operations are now performed at the same wages by workers of all races. These changes are important as showing a tendency for economic forces to dissolve the complex of the colour bar through the use of semi-skilled operatives. They also indicate the formation of an occupational urban pattern along the lines of the Western world. These tendencies have, however, not progressed very far. ' South African industries have been slow to make the fullest possible use of operative labour, which as a percentage of the total labour force is probably lower in the Union than in any other industrial country '.[1] Broadly speaking, it remains true that no important South African industry is composed of a labour force graded in remuneration, skill or type of operation, wholly in accordance with the technical requirements of the industry, or the capacity, output, efficiency, or other objective criteria of the worker's productivity.

The ' multi-racial team system ' of organizing labour is cumbersome in the extreme. It prevents the full development of latent income-creating power through specialization, appropriate incentives, and individual economic mobility. These are essential for the full unfolding of the modern forces of industrialism, and for the free development of personality on which alone they can be successfully based. It also disturbs the whole process of investment, and the organization of production in accordance with the most effective combination of capital and labour in the social interest. In consequence, the field of industrial relations in the Union is a mass of inconsistencies with avoidable surpluses of labour in some directions and often grave shortages of labour in others. The general picture which emerges is that of a society standing half-way between a feudal, or patriarchal organization of effort, on the one hand, and a modern open economic society, on the other hand.

The emergence of the open economic society in the Union is, however, not only arrested by feudal or racial conceptions. Many of the existing barriers to the full unfolding of human effort take the form of restrictive practices by particular sections of workers. These thereby endeavour

[1] Report No. 282 of the Board of Trade and Industries, para. 414.

to protect themselves against, or to enrich themselves by preventing, economic changes which would be in the interests of the community as a whole. Such practices have much more in common with anti-social trade union, guild or other monopolistic restrictions of a kind well known in the economic history of, or existing practices in, Western Europe than with racial prejudices which have resulted from the peculiar history of South Africa.

In my opinion, the most important task now facing the Union is that of conducting an objective, independent, and expert inquiry into the following questions :—

(1) The effect of the present organization of South Africa's economic life and labour on the productivity of the country.

(2) What alterations in existing forms of economic organization would increase productivity, would raise the National Income, and, while at least maintaining existing high income standards, would raise those of the economically backward sections of the community.

(3) The effect on different races, classes of workers, and producers of any changes in economic organization which may be found necessary or desirable.

(4) The practical measures which may be necessary to compensate or assist those races, classes of workers, and producers who may be detrimentally affected by economic changes required to raise the incomes of the under-developed sections of the community, while ensuring the maintenance of those higher incomes consonant with the aspirations of modern civilization.

I would draw particular attention to the third and fourth points of what might be called an 'Agenda of Objective Inquiry ' : they express the crucial economic problem of South Africa.

The Europeans in South Africa have throughout their history raised the standards of the indigenous peoples, not through the work of temporary residents, who return after a while to a metropolitan country across the seas, but by constructing a new modern society in the midst of, and with the help of, the native peoples.

I believe that the unfolding economic history of South Africa may well contain constructive lessons of great importance for the modern world which is still excessively preoccupied with the belief that the economic progress of underdeveloped societies must proceed on exclusively nationalistic lines.

The existence of a permanent European population, with high economic and cultural aspirations, has been the main cause of the relatively rapid economic advance of the indigenous peoples of South Africa. South Africa's problem is how to maintain and increase income standards all round, instead of diluting those already achieved. This is a problem which can be solved neither by a stroke of the pen nor by the power of the sword. It is a problem of modifying old and creating new institutions, a problem of change and a problem of assistance to those detrimentally affected by change, a problem of growth and social experimentation, rather than of dogmatic ideologies.

VII. ECONOMIC SOLIDARITY IN A MULTI-RACIAL SOCIETY

I am aware that there are some who might object to the assumptions on which this suggested inquiry is based. They might argue, especially, that in a multi-racial society there can be no general interest, but only the particular warring interests of its diverse racial groups. I disagree with this view for reasons which I cannot develop on this occasion, but which I have analysed elsewhere.[1] I will confine myself to stating that, in my view, there now exists an objective world economic solidarity, which is an inescapable reality and affects the lives of individuals in every community on the globe. Salvador de Madariaga has defined this objective aspect of world economic solidarity as ' The interdependence between parts of a whole, without which the whole does not exist '[2] This world economic solidarity exists whether we like it or not, but there is a distinction between it and our subjective

[1] Cf. S. Herbert Frankel : ' World Economic Solidarity ' and ' World Economic Welfare ', *South African Journal of Economics*, September 1942, and September 1943, vols. 10 and 11, respectively.

[2] Salvador de Madariaga : *Theory and Practice in International Relations*, page 5. (Oxford University Press, 1937).

solidarity, the solidarity which we feel and create by an active attitude of our mind and soul. For the full realization of the benefits of world economic solidarity the subjective appreciation of that solidarity must enter into the consciousness of the peoples of the world.

If it is true that the world as a whole is indeed an economic unity, and that perhaps nothing is more important for the future of all of us than a realization of this truth, how much more justified is it to postulate an objective economic solidarity in any particular country, no matter how racially diverse may be the composition of its inhabitants, and to stress the necessity of a subjective realization of this inescapable fact.

Indeed, there is no single part of the multi-racial society of South Africa which can afford to be oblivious to the direction and rate of movement of the society as a whole.

As I see the position, the Union now stands before greater opportunities than ever before in her history. The constructive forces of industrialism have advanced further within her borders than in any other territory in Africa. A new generation of men and women is emerging from her schools and universities, equipped as never before to grapple with South African problems. Her technicians and scientists as well as her industrialists and business men, are called to new tasks beyond the borders of the Union. They have already played a vital role, not only in the development of mining, agriculture, commerce and industry in other African territories, but also in grappling with the common problems of the environment of this rapidly unfolding continent. Moreover, in the last twenty-five years great advances have been made in dealing with the educational and sociological problems of its diverse peoples : a larger proportion of these than anywhere else in Africa has benefited from the contact with and the discipline of modern economic processes.

Yet notwithstanding the great economic tasks which the Union has already performed in developing its backward inhabitants, there is a very great danger that, owing to the economic windfalls resulting from the war and the new mining discoveries, the dragging effects of the outworn system of labour organization will again be overlooked, and that consequently the country will be unable to realize those very opportunities which have encouraged the striking spirit of economic enterprise which now exists.

Already there are signs that the Union is in imminent danger of a permanent slowing down of the rate of growth of, and even of a decline in, its productive powers, if these continue to be based on that institutional framework which now governs the organization of its working force.

Even immigration, which is still as essential as previously in the history of the Union, cannot in itself be relied upon to safeguard a continuous rate of economic expansion. Indeed, the flow of new immigrants is itself most seriously hampered by this ' multi-racial team system ' of labour organization which places serious obstacles in the way of the employment of any but specialist immigrant workers. It makes the numbers for whom employment can be found dependent not on their potentially diverse contributions, but on the places which can be found for them in the peculiar labour structure of the country.

There are other significant signs that the Union cannot cope effectively with its growing economic responsibilities. For the real meaning of the desperate struggle against poverty of a large part of the urban proletariat, both black and white, is that, although its money income is higher than previously, its efforts have not yet been so organized as to yield the much higher living standards required by an urban industrial working force. The need to house, feed, clothe, and educate this continuously growing urban population throws a tremendous strain on the Union's economy.

The strain in the towns is paralleled by a strain in the country, where agriculture is faced with the need for a radical change in its customary organization of work and life if it is to keep pace with the new demands made upon it for food and raw materials by the requirements of an improving national standard of nutrition on the one hand, and by world changes in agricultural techniques on the other hand.

In mining, the strain is clearly visible in the steady rise in gold-mining costs, which come up against the ceiling of a fixed price for gold over which the Union has no influence. Apart from monetary factors, the basic cause of this rise in cost lies in the rigid labour structure of the industry. Indeed, as I see the position, the full development of the newly-discovered gold-fields may be most seriously hampered, and the life of many existing mines unnecessarily curtailed, if these rigidities are not dealt with on their economic merits. The same strain on labour resources is reflected in manufacturing industry by the inability to compete more effectively in world markets.

VIII. THE CHALLENGE

Here then are objective problems which challenge all classes and all sections in the Union. Their solution is as vital to employers as to employees, to producers as to consumers, to one race as to another. They constitute the supreme challenge of South Africa's natural and human environment—a challenge which the Union must meet, and which cannot be escaped by taking merely momentary advantage of good fortune : which is as liable to obscure basic economic realities as misfortune will ruthlessly expose them in all their nakedness.

On the extent to which the Union succeeds in grappling with these problems will depend not only such mundane matters as the rate of growth of the National Income, but the role which the Union will play in the rest of Africa, to which it is already imparting so much, and could impart so much more. On it will depend, finally, the contribution of the Union to the common problems of the Commonwealth and the World.

' China,' wrote Adam Smith,[1] ' seems to have been long stationary, and had probably long ago acquired that full complement of riches which is consistent with the nature of its laws and institutions. But this complement may be much inferior to what, with other laws and institutions, the nature of its soil, climate, and situation might admit of '. In the same terms, it might be said that the fundamental need in the Union is for its people to awaken to a realization of what ' with other laws and institutions ', the natural and human resources of their country might admit of.

In the last resort, the future of the Union thus depends

---

[1] Adam Smith : *The Wealth of Nations.* Chapter IX.

upon the power of those with whom decision rests, to make not merely economic, but rather new moral decisions. In saying this I do not have in mind the application of a ready-made or absolute moral yard-stick—as if the problem involved were simply that of questioning the moral worth of the people of the Union. That is a too simple, even if at times a very popular method of escaping from reality. The men and women of South Africa on whom the responsibility for decision in these questions now rests are no better and no worse than other men and women who compose the human family of nations and societies. Like these they are encompassed by fears and doubts—some peculiar to their own environment and history, others which they share with their fellow-men across the seas. Their problem, like those of other peoples, is to disentangle right from wrong, and to illumine the consequences of fear-impelled social action by the fearless light of reason based on social justice and greater human understanding. As Professor Ginsberg has recently written :[1] 'In a changing and highly complex society the moral problems that arise require for their solution very often not so much fresh moral insight as a scientific analysis of the situation which might render possible the application of known principles. . . . Similarly, the problem of justice between nations or social classes is often intractable, not so much on account of the obscurity of the moral principles involved, but rather because of the difficulty of calculating in advance the consequences of the different lines of policy that are possible, especially the remote consequences. In any event, even if a divergence of moral principles be involved, the rational solution of a social conflict requires in addition to moral insight and the will to act on it an exact knowledge of the objective conditions of adjustment and thus a combination of ethics with physical and social science.'

It is in this sense that I conclude that the future of South Africa depends mainly on objective inquiry, and a supreme will to act on the results thereof, into those fundamental problems of economic organization which have been allowed to lie too long under the shadow of fear and doubt. I believe

[1] Morris Ginsberg : *Moral Progress. Being the Frazer Lecture delivered within the University of Glasgow*, 1944, page 28. (Jackson, Son and Company, Glasgow).

that if these problems are resolutely attacked the Union is likely to experience an era of development greater than any in her past, and that the peoples of South Africa have no reason to believe that they cannot cope with them nobly in the interests of the Union, of Africa, and of the World.

ESSAY VII

INVESTMENT AND ECONOMIC DEVELOPMENT IN THE CONTINENT OF AFRICA

I. INTRODUCTION

To endeavour to epitomize the problems of capital investment in a continent in a few pages must in itself be regarded as presumptuous ; to make the attempt when that continent is Africa, with its immense regional, political, and racial diversities, may well be foolhardy. In this essay I endeavour to focus attention on certain fundamental issues which are in some degree common to Africa south of the Sahara. This approach has obvious limitations. It precludes the detailed examination of trade, balance of payments, 'National Income', and similar economic indices for the separate territories ; of the differences in the rate of economic change in them ; of the great variations in population density in different areas ; and of the effects of population growth on the economic utilization of resources or on the break-down of particular systems of production.

I hope, however, in this way to contrast the basic nature of the investment problems with which the modern world is faced in Africa with those which now predominantly engage the attention of economists in the highly industrialized economies of Europe and America. In these latter attention has, in our generation, been increasingly concentrated on problems of investment in relation to anti-cyclical policy. In a continent, however, most of whose indigenous peoples had, for better or for worse, little more than a generation ago never experienced any of the so-called blessings of modern economic organization, not to speak of the social heritage—technological, scientific, or cultural—of the West, and whose views, if any, on ' social security ' were necessarily concerned rather with avoiding enslavement and the ravages of inter-tribal warfare, famine, or disease, than with the problems of the ' Welfare State ', it is not perhaps surprising that disputation about saving, income, and employment, and their

K

cyclical fluctuations, does not command the same priority of attention as in the conference halls of Europe and America, or in the classrooms of their universities.

In Africa we have to examine the problems of capital investment and accumulation, and the role of capital itself, in more basic, and indeed more ' human ', terms. In societies in which neither social beliefs, nor economic behaviour patterns, nor the process of investment—that is, of economic decisions to apply or combine economic resources in a certain manner for the future—nor its consequences, can be taken as given, there is little one can take for granted. Moreover, many of the more refined procedures of statistical analysis are not as yet very helpful in Africa owing to the inconvenient fact that so far no one has been able to collect statistics of the unknown, far less to interpret them; and Africa is indeed still to a far greater extent than many imagine the Unknown Continent.

II. The Economic Framework

Human societies picture the future in terms of past experience. It is therefore not surprising that the European colonizing powers, as I endeavoured to show elsewhere,[1] originally thought of their task of pacifying and opening up the continent very much in terms of investment in railways, roads, and communications which, it was hoped, would, as was the case in America, pave the way for the migration into an ' empty ' continent of European peoples who would ' naturally ' proceed to develop its resources. The construction of a basic framework of communications was in any case an inescapable burden. It was necessary for strategic and administrative reasons ; without it the African continent south of the Sahara would have remained as closed to the world economy as it had been almost since the dawn of history.

Most of this basic framework of modern administration and economic intercourse had to be paid for by investment from abroad in the form of government grants, loans, military expenditures, and the like. Private investors did not, and

---

[1] *Capital Investment in Africa. Its Course and Effects*, Oxford University Press, 1938.

could not have been expected to undertake the task : the individual net product was insufficient, and was never expected to be other than insufficient, to meet the current yields demanded by investors.

It is significant that of the total capital invested in Africa from 1870 to 1936 nearly one-half was supplied by governments or public authorities. Of the remainder a large part has been connected with mining and exploration activities, especially gold-mining ; in these directions the individual net product to private enterprise was expected to be considerable, or, at any rate, speculatively attractive.[1]

The construction of the modern economic framework did not, however, for political, economic, and climatic reasons, bring with it the expected large migration of European peoples with their social and psychological heritage of modern industrialism. On the contrary, the foundation of all modern economic development was provided by the psychologically, socially, and economically unadjusted labour of its indigenous peoples.

This led to the development of a peculiar pattern of economic production. Its characteristic feature is the employment of a relatively very large proportion of unskilled, undifferentiated, indigenous labour. This tends to be increasingly divorced from employment on the land, and even from residence on it, with a consequent continuous increase in urbanization. Mining enterprises in Africa typify the pattern of production which characterizes economic evolution in Africa under the impact of investment from abroad : in them is exposed, in an extreme form, the economic dilemma which the modern world now faces in Africa.

As is well known, whenever the agencies utilizing capital from abroad, be they government or private, have to make direct or indirect provision for servicing the debts so incurred or for providing the foreign investor with a sufficient yield on equity capital to ensure that further supplies of it will be made available, the development of industries exploiting mineral

---

[1] In all speculations the individual winners are, fortunately or unfortunately, usually unaware of the extent of the losses of those who are unsuccessful. The overall yield to the capital invested in mining enterprise in Africa illustrates this very forcibly. Africa has in one sense profited much from the over-optimism usually displayed by gamblers.

and other natural resources for export is inevitable. This in effect means that the economy, having undertaken the capital investment to provide the basic modern economic framework to which I have referred, must, unless there is very considerable migration which provides the whole range of the required complementary labour and skill from abroad, detach labour from the indigenous social pattern of tribal economic organization. It will perforce have to use it in those directions which will yield exports to meet the external payments obligations, as well as to pay for imports not covered by investment from abroad. Indeed, it will need to detach labour from the indigenous economic structure even for carrying out the original capital construction of the framework, and it will be forced in general to engage in those types of production which will be expected to yield immediately the greatest individual net product. This is inescapable unless capital is made so 'cheap', i.e. is available for such long periods of time, in such amounts, and on such easy terms of debt service, that it is possible to use it for very long-run improvements in order to establish the modern pattern of economic activity. I have in mind improvements which will develop the efficiency or productivity of labour itself—using the term in its widest sense to include organizational, managerial, or entrepreneurial ability. I also have in mind improvements to 'land and natural resources', for example, new or more suitable types of plant and animal life, soil conservation, water supplies, and the like.

To illustrate this I would ask you, momentarily, to enter with me into the realm of fancy. Let us imagine that capital were to be supplied from abroad as a free good in unlimited quantities. That would, of course, mean that as far as the indigenous peoples were concerned they could (if we make the far-reaching assumption that they wished to do so) proceed unhampered to adopt Western industrial civilization; and to remould it nearer to their hearts' desires in the course of its transplantation to Africa. They could devote their time to acquiring proficiency in new pursuits, to evolving new methods of agriculture and industry, to planning and building modern cities, and to preparing themselves, their children, and their children's children for their chosen new way of life.

They would be able to take *unlimited* time in realizing the new heaven on earth—since meanwhile they could be fed, housed, educated, and generally equipped for it by unlimited supplies of food and other consumer's necessities : these and the machinery and equipment needed for construction purposes would be paid for by the gifts of Fairy Godmother 'Dame Capital', who might possibly reside in Washington in the Headquarters of the 'Point Four' Administration. We cannot, however, be certain that they would necessarily so use her gifts. It might well happen, if history were to repeat itself, that while the less popular ' Dame Necessity ', the Mother of Invention, was busy looking over her shoulder they might prefer to sit for too long, under the shadow of the proverbial African palm-tree, in deep contemplation of the past which alone they know.

But let us proceed. The moral of this fanciful story is, of course, that the line between capital and the whole ' heritage of improvement ' is not and never can be a hard and fast one. As Cannan pointed out,[1] capital is not the whole of that man-made heritage. In common usage the term capital was, in the past, generally applied to purchasable and saleable private, and more recently to ' public ', property. It used to exclude things not openly sold for and bought with money. This use of the term suffers from serious disadvantages into which I do not wish to enter here, except to say that when there is a *change* from one type of economic and social organization and *way of life* to another, society may require resources to enable it to support itself during the process of transition and while it is engaged on acquiring the new social heritage : resources so utilized are as much ' capital ' as are machinery or factory buildings or other kinds of ' saleable ' property. Such resources might consist of food imports, to enable a part of the society in question to devote itself to scientific research, to experimentation, to teaching, or to acquiring new skills in administration or industry.

Unfortunately in the real world financial Fairy Godmothers are rare. Consequently the *immediately possible* pattern of economic activity involves the employment of the types of labour and those natural resources which are at hand, or can

---

[1] ' Capital and the Heritage of Improvement,' *Economica*, London, Nov. 1934.

be very soon brought into combination, in order to yield a sufficient and not long-deferred net product. The need to resort to such combinations of the factors as are immediately possible has grave consequences : there results from such combinations a particular pattern of economic activity which tends to perpetuate itself, and to become ever more rigidly established. It creates its own vested interests and makes difficult the establishment of other forms of combination of resources. Indeed, it may lead to the establishment of legal and social sanctions specifically designed to prevent any change which will alter the production pattern itself.

Such sanctions already permeate the whole of the South African economy.[1] They have as their object the perpetuation of supplies of labour of that undifferentiated and unskilled type on which the ' modern ' economic pattern of production was first erected. Many examples of this process, both in Africa and elsewhere, readily spring to mind. Thus in British Guiana it was, in an earlier period, a criminal offence to grow rice at a time when it was being imported, from as far as India and Burma, to feed the Indian immigrants; it was feared that rice-growing would lead to the deflection of labour from the sugar plantations.[2]

III. The Dilemma of Development

This tendency lies at the root of the dilemma of African development to which I have referred. For in all African territories the development of modern methods of economic organization is in greater or lesser degree accompanied by increasingly rapid disintegration of the indigenous economic and social structure. However primitive those indigenous institutions may now appear to Western eyes, they did in fact provide the individuals composing the indigenous society with that sense of psychological and economic security without which life loses its meaning.

Of course, all economic development involves a process of disintegration of previous patterns of economic

[1] Cf. Essay No. VI in this volume.
[2] See G. B. Masefield : *A Short History of Agriculture in the British Colonies*, Oxford University Press, 1950.

cohesion. But whereas in the highly industrialized countries of Europe and America we have come to take for granted—far too readily, I fear—this process of disintegration and subsequent reintegration of the ' factors of production ' into new and ' better ' combinations (assuming the ' right ' decisions of policy by private or public entrepreneurial agencies), in Africa we take any such process for granted at our peril. For in Africa, as we have seen, the factors of production cannot be assumed to be ready for recombination. They are highly specific to particular ways of life and work which had achieved equilibrium within a narrowly circumscribed ecological and human environment; they are not, as a rule, easily combined into new patterns of production. On the contrary, they tend to be recombined into patterns of activity which may give rise to grave problems of social and economic instability, and may eventually involve comparatively heavy social and economic costs, just because there is no time for the slower evolution necessary for stable integration into a new economic and social whole.

This time period of preparation is, of course, but another name for the supply of the necessary subsistence or capital fund on which the community can draw, in its transition from the old to the new. Without the expenditure of ' capital ' on its improvement most African labour can only be used at present for its physical brawn. It cannot be utilized in any other economic capacity. But such capital expenditure, for example on re-education and re-location, involves vast changes in ' consumer habits '. The whole way of life of the people concerned is affected—their diet, the ' protective ' clothing they require, the housing suited to their new urban conditions, and a large range of other needs which must be met, for physiological and psychological reasons, to ensure the social health and economic efficiency of the transplanted community.

In the first round of development the new society is not burdened with all these social or capital costs : the modern sectors of the economy can make use of migrant labour, i.e. of labour not fully detached from its indigenous economic structure. But such a system of migrant labour finally leads to the undermining of the rural economy, which serves as its base, owing to the progressive deterioration of the whole social and economic life of the indigenous structure as it is drained of its able-bodied and more enterprising members. The labour force becomes progressively detribalized : finally the modern sector of the economy has to provide for the whole social and capital cost of maintaining a large, and relatively unskilled, urban proletariat. If urbanization, and the destruction of the rural economy, proceeds rapidly, the process may even destroy a considerable part of the previous 'subsistence' production, and of the man-made improvements in the indigenous economy. That subsistence production is, of course, bound in any case to prove inadequate to supply the food and other agricultural requirements of the new urban population. Consequently the economy comes to be faced with the need for developing new patterns of agricultural production, and has to shoulder the burden of the additional capital costs thereof ; it may, indeed, have to save the land itself from erosion and other forms of deterioration. In this connexion it must always be remembered that the indigenous rural economy has neither the knowledge and skill, nor the capital to initiate these changes itself—even if the physical labour resources which remain on the land are sufficient for the purpose.

The short-fall in food production can be made good by imports which, unless paid for by greater exports (which would of course lead to an even more rapid disintegration), would have to be financed by capital from abroad. Yet even this latter alternative is, apart from the capital costs involved, not at all as simple a process as might appear to be the case. It, too, requires considerable changes in food-habits, tastes, and distributive organization—which may require a long time to bring about.

It is on account of the increasing rapidity of the process of disintegration to which I have referred that there have been growing demands in all African territories for greater expenditures on 'Welfare'. A very large part of these expenditures simply reflect the unavoidable social capital costs of change, which have to be borne, either equally or unequally, within the community, unless the human suffering which change involves can be mitigated by gifts, or not too burdensome capital investment from abroad.

In the Union of South Africa the dilemma of disintegration is most clearly visible because industrialization has there proceeded farther than elsewhere in Africa. The gap between the inadequately equipped indigenous proletariat and the demands of modern production for skilled labour and entrepreneurial activity is filled by the European middle and artisan classes. By reason of the original scarcity of the types of services which they supply they have been able to entrench themselves in an economic position which yields them a relatively high standard of life; and prevents others from attaining it. Although confronted with the vast costs of urbanization and the growing need for rural rehabilitation, these entrenched classes are not psychologically prepared to break the fetters of the original production pattern. In this connexion it is very significant that, broadly speaking, the economy is still relatively as dependent on extractive industry, and on capital from abroad to finance it, as it was at the beginning of the century.

It may be thought that the economy of the Union is, after all, only a special case, owing to the existence of a relatively large settled European population. But such a view obscures the real nature of the dilemma of disintegration, however much racial and economic discrimination is to be deplored. For even when this is absent ' the barrier of time ' still remains throughout Africa, whether it be in mines or plantations, in private factories, or in public enterprises : any rapid economic change leads to the disintegration of indigenous society—even where there is no permanent European population.

Thus the African peoples are themselves caught up in the vicious dilemma of change. They fear the creation of a situation such as that which exists in the Union of South Africa, and consequently mistrust not only the importation of skilled economic leadership from abroad, but even the creation of a new class of economic leaders at home. Yet, while distrusting and fearing change, many desire its fruits and wish to benefit from the life and thought of the modern world—often oblivious to the large social and economic costs thereof in relation to their meagre resources.

Given therefore the need for capital to promote change, how is it to be obtained and how can it be applied without the development of structural patterns of economic activity which disrupt the old, yet do not build new stable economic and social relations? That is the question which faces Africa and the world. Here I cannot attempt to do more than pose the question.

IV. THE CLIMATE OF INVESTMENT

It remains to consider how the psychology of investment from the standpoint of those supplying capital from abroad has been affected by the vast changes that have taken place in Europe since the turn of the century. It is well to remember that the climate of opinion in which the great speculative investments in Africa took place, when Europe was the world's banker, has suffered a sea change. Gone are the days when the opening up of Africa could be looked upon as a natural part of Europe's economic and financial expansion. Gone is the easy belief that, given only communications, order, and 'good' government, Africa's natural resources would automatically yield an adequate return to those supplying equity capital for their development. The supply of risk capital is at a premium in Europe itself. The complex financial structure, with its far-reaching personal links and experience, built up by a generation of venturesome European investors in relation to Africa, has not yet been created in other capital markets on which Africa might draw. It may indeed never again be built on the pattern of the past.

Nor is the continuous supply of capital by the governments of European powers, or their agencies, more certain. Quite apart from the fact that the available supplies of such capital are by no means permanently assured, there are new factors of importance which have only become apparent recently. Firstly, there is the fact that much of the capital now needed in Africa is for purposes other than the construction of that economic framework to which I have earlier referred. To an increasing extent it has become necessary for governments to endeavour to finance enterprises which in one form or another could previously be left to private enterprise. But the institutions and experience for this new kind of investment are still lacking.

Secondly, there is the fact that European colonial powers no longer exercise sovereignty to the same extent as previously: the existence of legal and constitutional safeguards for private persons, or for governments themselves, in relation to investment in African territories previously under their rule, can no longer be taken for granted. African nationalism carries with it all the usual dangers which foreign governments or nationals have to fear from the unpredictable policies of sovereign nation states.

Thirdly, the very social and economic disruption to which we have referred is making the future course of economic development in Africa, and its political repercussions, more uncertain. Latent tensions are being released which may affect not only the productivity of capital itself but the willingness of external investors—public or private—to become involved in them.

Thus one can sum up by saying that the problem of economic development in Africa has in fact ceased to be, if it ever was, a narrow economic question : it is a question of incorporating Africa into the world economy at a rate, and in a manner, which will not endanger the peace and political stability of Africa itself.

Africa has become a problem of world statesmanship : the 'White Man's Burden' has become the burden of the free world in much more than metaphorical terms. For as long as we can foresee, Africa alone will not be able to provide even a small fraction of the economic and technical framework required to make it a more effective part of the work and life of the outside world. Much patient and persistent effort will be required to create new international, financial, economic, and administrative institutions for the development of the productivity of its peoples.

It is also clear that capital investment in and by itself is not the answer to Africa's economic problems : far greater attention has to be devoted to the particular institutional manner in which it is supplied, and used, so as to ensure that it will meet the need which perhaps dominates all else—the need to fashion new economic structures which will prove to be socially stable.

Whether in these circumstances capital can be supplied in sufficient amounts, and, if so, how it can be effectively mobilized in a continent so ill equipped with a complementary social heritage of production, and so burdened with ecological and environmental difficulties, we do not yet know. In that ignorance lies the challenge of Africa to the freely creative world.

THE KONGWA EXPERIMENT:
LESSONS OF THE EAST AFRICAN GROUND-NUT SCHEME

I. Introductory Note

At the end of the Second World War the shortage of fats and animal feeding stuffs presented the British Government and people with a problem of extreme difficulty.

Because of this a plan was laid before the British Government by Mr. Frank Samuel, the Managing Director of the United Africa Company. Mr. Samuel suggested that in East Africa there might be scope for the mechanized production of groundnuts on a large scale.

An official mission was therefore sent to East Africa under the leadership of Mr. A. J. Wakefield, and on September 20th, 1946, it presented its report to the Secretary of State for the Colonies. He and his colleagues confidently supported the project and subject to minor modifications recommended its immediate adoption. The following is a brief survey of the salient developments in the history of the project, and has been compiled from the official reports of the Overseas Food Corporation.

On November 25th, two months after the Mission's report had been presented, the Minister of Food informed the House of Commons that the Government had decided to proceed with the Scheme to accept the Mission's proposed programme for 1947, but to delay any decision about the full scope of the plan until there had been more time to consider it. In fact on November 6th, 1946, at the invitation of the Minister of Food, the United Africa Company (Managing Agency) Ltd., took charge of the start of the enterprise. The plan was the plan contained in the report of the Mission, but which had been modified in certain respects by the Ministry of Food.

While operations for the first year were put in hand, a further and much more detailed examination of the plans for subsequent years was made; and in February 1947 their final decision was printed in the form of a White Paper entitled 'A Plan for the Mechanized Production of Groundnuts in East and Central Africa ', Cmd. 7030 (which is the document discussed in this essay). The Government's view expressed therein was that ' the Scheme is a practicable plan for alleviating the world shortage of fats, which is likely to last for many years ; that it is agriculturally sound ; that subject to reasonable assumptions, it involves no unjustifiable risk ; that labour difficulties can be overcome . . . and that it could prove of great benefit to the African populations as well as to the people of the United Kingdom '. It should be noted that this plan was much larger in scope than that suggested originally.

At the end of January 1947 the advance party from the Managing Agency and the Contractors arrived in Dar-es-Salaam and the work began. The Kongwa area of the Central Province was selected by the Managing Agents as the scene for the most intensive effort in preference to the Southern Province, or Urambo. In the autumn of 1947 Mr. Plummer and General Harrison visited Tanganyika. As an outcome of this visit the Overseas Food Corporation at the request of the Minister of Food took over the responsibility for the direction of the East African Groundnuts Scheme on March 1st, 1948.

The Corporation, on taking over administrative control on April 1st, 1948, considered it necessary to revise the original plan (Cmd. 7030), and a revised plan was approved and announced in the House of Commons on November 21st, 1949.

The year 1949–50 was on the whole disappointing. And the further disappointing agricultural results at Kongwa for the second year in succession led the Overseas Food Corporation to appoint a Working Party, with the following terms of reference.

' To recommend the long-term and short-term agricultural policies to be pursued by the Corporation in the Kongwa Region in the light of the results achieved to date and other evidence.'

The Working Party, consisting of Sir Charles Lockhart, Professor J. F. V. Phillips, Mr. G. F. Clay, Dr. H. H. Storey, Professor S. H. Frankel, Mr. A. M. B. Hutt and Mr. J. C.

Muir, in effect recommended that the project for the large-scale mechanized production of groundnuts should be abandoned.

In Paragraph 16 of this report (dated August 18th, 1950) it stated :

'Our consideration of all the evidence presented to us in relation to this aspect of the problem has led us to conclude :

(*a*) That the Corporation would be ill-advised to proceed in 1950–51 with large scale agriculture at Kongwa on the lines adopted in 1949–50.

(*b*) That the attempt to establish a pattern of arable agriculture suitable to the cleared area (which has been created at a great cost and may be a potential asset of importance) should not be abandoned without further experiments on a field scale ; the total scale being limited to approximately 24,000 acres, with arable cultivation of 12,000 acres annually.'

The essay below was published in the form of two articles in *The Times* on October 4th and 5th, 1950. I wrote these articles in order to draw attention to certain fundamental economic principles which my experience on the Working Party led me to believe had been overlooked when the project was first embarked upon. The articles deal with theoretical considerations ; these were outside the strict confines of the terms of reference of the Working Party ; they were not therefore dealt with by it or incorporated in its report. I wish to stress that in writing these articles I was not concerned with, nor did I ever concern myself with, questions of personal responsibility for the final formulation and implementation of the various plans which it was attempted to put into effect at Kongwa.

It was also not my intention to suggest that either Mr. Frank Samuel or the United Africa Company, (Managing Agency) Ltd. during its very brief period of management of the scheme, were responsible for the disappointing results at Kongwa. In examining some of the fundamental concepts and assumptions of the original plan for producing ground-nuts in Tanganyika, Northern Rhodesia, and Kenya,[1] I was

---

[1] *A Plan for the Mechanized Production of Groundnuts in East and Central Africa*, Feb. 1947. Cmd. 7030.

not concerned with the detailed administration of the scheme, or with any information which had not been published. It cannot, in my opinion, be too strongly emphasized, however, that those who were asked to implement the plan were unable at any time to escape from the fundamental concepts on which it was originally based. Whatever mistakes were made were due primarily to the nature of the task, not to the men who had to try to carry it out, and who, indeed, laboured with great zeal, determination, and much self-sacrifice.

II. EXTENT OF THE PROJECT

At the outset I wish to isolate some of the processes of thought behind, and certain lessons to be learnt from, this extraordinary project. The word 'extraordinary' is used advisedly because it is difficult for anyone, be he expert or layman in agricultural matters, to conceive the magnitude of the project which was so enthusiastically and hastily adopted. It will be remembered that the scheme, as set out in the report of the Wakefield Mission, provided for the development of 107 units, each of 30,000 acres, of which 80 units were to be in Tanganyika Territory, 17 units in Northern Rhodesia, and 10 units in Kenya. The total area involved was thus 3,210,000 acres, one half of which was envisaged as being under cultivation at any one time. In other words, the scheme involved the creation of what can only be described as whole counties or provinces of continuous arable agriculture, complete with drainage systems, roads, and anti-erosion earthworks of the project.

Some conception of its vastness is revealed by the remark of one of America's foremost agricultural experts, who on looking out from a small hill at Kongwa, confessed that he was experiencing the greatest thrill of his life because there was spread before him the largest continuous area of mechanized arable land in the world. Yet he was then able to see little more than one of the three units of 30,000 acres which had been cleared. A total of 450,000 acres was to have been cleared at Kongwa, but, as is now well-known, less than a quarter of this target was achieved and at no time was all of this reduced acreage cultivated according to plan.

The essence of the proposals affirmed that it was possible, desirable, and indeed urgently necessary, to do in five years what might normally be expected to take a generation or more. The reason for the belief in the possibility of so rapidly conquering the inevitable handicaps of time was based on a peculiar view of the process of economic development : namely, that capital can do anything ; that it is only the lack of capital on the one hand, and of human volition on the other, which prevent human societies from converting a desert into an agricultural paradise.

It would be unfair to blame the authors of the project entirely for this peculiar notion. It is one which lies at the root of a considerable part of even serious modern economic writing, particularly on the nature of investment. To those holding such views, which are based on the facile mechanistic concept that economic evolution is determined mainly by the application of technical power, time always appears as the enemy, never as the ally, of man.

True to the spirit of our age the report of the Wakefield Mission is grandiose in its ambitions and regards their attainment as merely a question of will. Thus in submitting the report its authors wrote (italics are mine) :

' We are confident that the project for the *mass* production of groundnuts is a practicable one, and that if the necessary staff and heavy field equipment is forthcoming when required, the territories of Tanganyika, Northern Rhodesia and Kenya could attain, *within a period of five years*, an annual production of 600,000 tons of groundnuts . . . we have no doubt that, *given the will*, this target figure could be vastly exceeded in course of time.'

Indeed they declared, in Section 1 of paragraph 2 on page 18, that

' *No significant increase* in the present output of oilseeds can be achieved, however, by the existing methods of peasant production. *Nothing but the most highly mechanised agricultural methods, on a vast scale never previously envisaged*, will result in any appreciable amelioration of the present disastrous food position.'

Moreover, not only were they convinced that the large capital investment in mechanization would inevitably be

L

successful, but to them ' time was of the essence ' and they clearly regarded the large capital investment as a means of ' buying time '. So imbued in fact was the Mission with the magic properties of capital that it completed its work ' in a little over nine weeks only, by recourse to aerial reconnaissance of the many thousands of square miles of land involved ', covering over 10,000 miles by air, 2,000 miles by road, and 1,000 miles by rail. It is significant, therefore, that before work was commenced at Kongwa no time could be spared for satisfactory and sustained primary reconnaissance and survey, for preliminary photographic work, for topographic soil conservation and soil maps, for adequate investigation of meteorological information bearing on rainfall, or even for an adequate examination of the economic aspects of crop yields.

III. MANPOWER ILLUSION

Not only time, however, but African man himself was regarded as an obstacle. Unbelievable as this may seem, the Report throughout regards the absence of population as a veritable advantage. In paragraph 11 it actually stressed that

'Areas of sparse population, unencumbered by native or other rights, are necessary if operations are to be started quickly. *Uninhabited, tsetse-infected and waterless areas therefore offer special attraction to the project, provided the soil is suitable* and rainfall adequate ; this type of country is almost limitless in Tanganyika and Northern Rhodesia.'

What is remarkable is the extraordinary assumption that mechanization, to be successful, must be total—that it must have as its objective the maximum elimination of man himself as co-worker. Indeed the Mission regarded as an advantage that when the clearing programme for the 3,210,000 acres had been completed in 1953 (of which 1,605,000 acres would have been planted) there would only be employed in this vast area 32,100 Africans and 749 Europeans and that no seasonal labour would be required.

Yet the very first objective of any development project in these Central African regions should surely have been to discover, through careful experimentation, what would best constitute an economically balanced farming system—that is to discover the most economic manner in which man's efforts could be combined with the services of the machine to yield optimum economic results. The Mission, however, seems to have regarded the machine as having an economic power of its own and for the most part as alternative to, and not as supplementing man's efforts. Nor does the Mission appear to have been conscious of the over-riding fact that the machine, though technically a powerful aid, is usually a most costly factor of production—giving rise also to other direct and indirect costs—which makes its substitution for hand labour on a large scale in Africa economically and indeed even socially warranted only in special circumstances, and certainly only when expected crop yields and revenues are so high and regular over a period of years as to justify the large and rigid capital costs involved.

It is indeed significant that in the report it is nowhere recognized that large-scale mechanization designed to reduce man-power to a minimum might be uneconomic. Yet the world over, at the peaks of agricultural activity, such as planting, weeding or harvesting, almost every able-bodied inhabitant of an agricultural village is needed to reinforce the efforts of the machine, and, if one crop fails to become established, to help plant another. If this agricultural population is non-existent there has to be substituted a vast reserve of machines complete with skilled attendants. No agricultural enterprise, however, can bear the huge capital overheads which such mechanical reserve capacity—to take the place of all hand-labour in periods of emergency—would entail. The larger the scale of mechanization, the more likely it therefore becomes that emergencies will upset the whole plan of operations ; seed-beds may not be ready ; crops may not be replanted in time ; weeding may have to be forgone at a critical moment ; or harvesting may remain uncompleted because of the vagaries of the weather and the inability to adjust available equipment and technical staff to it in time. All this did happen at Kongwa owing to the extremely short season—of five to six weeks—in which agricultural operations preceding and including planting have to be completed. It is likely to happen whenever the fundamental interdependence of man and the environment he wishes to subdue are disregarded.

It is convenient at this point to draw attention to another fallacy which dominated the Report: its assumptions regarding labour requirements, which also disregarded the time factor. Far from the machine being a substitute for man, it lays an inexorable burden upon him, since without constant and skilled attention for both maintenance and operation it soon becomes a useless tool. In short, without a highly skilled industrial population to draw on—nonexistent in Africa—the machine easily becomes a liability rather than an asset.

The development of skill, however, is necessarily slow when the people concerned, as at Kongwa, are technically primitive and so far removed from understanding the new mechanical tools that when first confronted by them they took fright and ran away. Up to the present it has not been possible to obtain an adequately skilled native labour force, and in consequence the number of highly paid Europeans that has had to be employed at Kongwa has been completely uneconomic in relation to the productivity of this area.

IV. Failure of Machines

Not only the creation of the labour force, however, but the fashioning of machines is a slow evolutionary process—another point overlooked in the Report, which seems to have been dominated by the fallacy that the required machines were already invented, constructed, and ready for buying. In fact not only were new machines of established types not available in the desired quantities, with the consequence that all sorts of mechanical equipment had to be rummaged from the salvage dumps of the world, but it was soon found that even the new machines were technically unequal to the unique problems in East Africa. Their failure was attributed to the malignity of fate, or to accident; but it was of course once again the inevitable consequence of disregarding the time factor. For every new set of circumstances the right machine has to be invented or devised, which involves long and arduous experimentation, re-designing, further research, the creation of pilot machines and the like, as every industrialist knows to his cost. Often the attempts have finally to be abandoned, because although the new machine may at length be perfected its operation may prove uneconomic.

So that again we meet the basic fallacy that capital has merely to be invested in order to create income in the future. All that capital provides, however, is what the past has created. It cannot buy future time in any other sense than that it will aid men and women in exploring the future. The machine, like man himself, has to be re-created afresh, and indeed to be renewed from day to day. It is not ready at hand for new tasks. The tools of the past and the stocks of goods and equipment needed to maintain life in the present carry no certain guarantee of success in creating additional income in the unknown future.

Large-scale mechanization, moreover, requires not only a specialized human, but also a vast and highly expensive economic framework of roads, railways, power stations, and water supplies. In economically developed and diversified areas these indirect costs do not fall on a single enterprise but are shared between agriculture, mining, and industry. But in Central Africa and similar regions far removed from urban industry, production is concentrated on a very limited range of crops, which by themselves have to bear the whole of these indirect costs. Consequently, the greater the scale of operations and degree of mechanization, the more burden-some such costs become.

V. ECONOMIES OF SCALE

At this point it is well to consider what was perhaps the most fundamental assumption of the whole proposal—namely, that agricultural operations can be assumed to lend themselves to economies on a very large scale. This is a surprising assumption because it runs counter to the accepted principle that agriculture is generally the least likely form of economic enterprise to yield considerable large-scale economies ; its factors of production cannot be readily centred and super-vised, nor, in general, are they sufficiently homogeneous to allow easily organized repetitive processes of production.

It is this reliance on the expected economies of large-scale that possibly accounts for the Mission's perfunctory investigation of groundnut yields. It apparently arrived at its estimates by the extraordinary procedure of taking sample yields of native crops in selected localities and on small patches of land, and from various soils on experiment-stations in Northern Rhodesia and Uganda, and multiplying them by the total acreage to be planted on the large scale it recommended. It does not seem to have been clearly recognized that these yields did not represent adequate statistical sampling; that land cannot safely be regarded as a homogeneous factor of production over large areas ; that even if it were, the rain which fell on it would vary ; and that yields were therefore not to be calculated by such simple arithmetic as was unfortunately applied, not only in this instance, but in almost all the estimates which appeared in the Report, and which were subsequently found to be so very erroneous.

In reality all practical farming proceeds by experimenting with specific crops on relatively small areas ; which is one reason why farms in Africa are widely scattered over suitable areas. Large areas, equal in their economic, ecological, and biological characteristics are the exception and not the rule. Moreover, the agricultural conditions of both small and large areas, like the best mechanical equipment, can be discovered only by slow and arduous experimentation and long farming practice, based on almost day-to-day adaptation of man to the exigencies of the soil and climate. Attempts at uniform large-scale operations, except in areas which by rare good fortune are ecologically homogeneous, destroy this process of economic adaptation.

The Mission, however, proceeded on quite different lines. It concluded first ' that the production of groundnuts is immediately practicable over considerable areas . . . using methods already known to be sound ' (par. 53), adding that the application of scientific knowledge and research would lead both to considerable economies of effort and materials and to considerable increases in yield. From this it went on to recommend further research into almost every conceivable aspect of agricultural operations, soil conservation, seed selection, and the like. What is not clear, with so many unknowns requiring research, is how the Mission could so confidently have recommended the immediate implementation of proposals based largely on abstract reasoning. It quite overlooked the paradox that the research it recommended was to follow, not precede, the erection of the vast enterprise which it proposed. So that while the actual nature of economic farming operations, from the right type of seed to the right type and amount of fertilizer, had still to be discovered, the undertaking itself was to go full speed ahead, with a colossal capital and current expenditure, and no certainty of revenue. The Mission apparently never realized the full implication of the fact that costly research might have to be pursued for a quite unconscionable time before it yielded results—and, more important, that it might not yield successful results at all.

Space does not permit me to illustrate this point at length but, to take one example, we find the Mission, in paragraph 19, confidently asserting that ' the ill-effects of short droughts can be largely mitigated by the adoption of soil-conservation measures and the application of other principles of good farming '. Yet the exact nature of the soil-conservation measures which would be most *economical* and effective, and the good farming principles which would prove both technically and economically suitable to these areas, had still to be discovered.

Moreover it did not seem to have occurred to the Mission that its discoveries from research would probably involve important alterations to the whole plan of operations. Once a large-scale organization has been set up, however, it cannot easily be adapted to the lessons of experience, being set in rigid grooves from the outset. Its very situation, its network of roads, workshops, power stations, bore-holes, townships, and the like leave little room for organic re-adaptation in policy and objectives. Consequently when change can no longer be postponed it has to be unavoidably drastic ; suddenly—and usually too late—it is realized that much of the capital has been lost: that nothing further can be done with it except to write it off.

For example, the decision to commence operations at Kongwa—a waterless and sparsely populated area—had as a consequence that any considerable deviation from the assumed ratio of men to machines, any considerable shift of methods of peasant farming, or alteration to the pattern of operations by the introduction of hand labour, would later be most difficult, if not impossible. Even if the population could be made available, the absence of adequate water supplies would make permanent settlement a major problem.

To sum up, I would say that the scheme was, in the first instance, nothing more than an over-large land-clearing operation. It failed to allow for the long period of time which would elapse before knowledge and experience would indicate the most suitable scale and type of organization for economic production in the proposed regions. It took for granted that once the land had been cleared successful agriculture could be immediately established by large-scale mechanization. But nobody yet knows the scale or system of farming which can economically replace the primitive native efforts in these regions.

VI. ADVANCE AND RETREAT

That, however, should be regarded as a challenge—not as a cause for despair. Very large parts of the high-lying regions of Central Africa, from Northern Rhodesia to Northern Nigeria, consist of land climatically similar to that in Central Tanganyika, and the discovery of the correct unit for balanced farming on modern lines would be of untold significance for the future of Africa as a whole. That discovery must clearly not do violence to the fundamental principle of economic growth—slow alternate advance and retreat as experience dictates. Those who wish to obtain the fruits of economic enterprise must not regard it from the viewpoint of the obstinate gambler who sees the size of the prize as directly proportional to the amount he is willing to stake, oblivious to the fact that his ticket may not be the winning one!

On the contrary it is arguable that our experience in Africa shows the unknown variables to be so many, particularly in agriculture, that economic advance over most of the continent requires maximum flexibility and decentralization of authority in all experimental economic enterprises. Flexible experimentation in turn pre-supposes suitably small units adaptable to the diverse range of ecological, climatic and economic conditions. It is no accident that most successful economic enterprise in Africa has been the work of small groups of men, often individuals, battling for many years before finally triumphing over particular environmental problems—developing suitable crops, acclimatizing animal populations, and striking the right balance between arable and other types of farming.

It is of the very greatest importance that efforts to unlock the productive secret of these unutilized African lands are now being made. The fact that the problems which have to be faced have been over-simplified must not discourage further attempts at their solution. Government and semi-government agencies will continue to be confronted with the need to finance an expanding framework of communications, power resources, irrigation, land-clearing and the like. But, as this essay is intended to show, a new economic potential will not emerge if the construction of this wider framework is embarked upon precipitously in advance of the necessarily more gradual growth of knowledge, of experience, and of the social, communal and educational factors which all permanent advance involves. It is of the utmost importance that every effort should be made to establish viable economic units, be they arable, pastoral, or a combination of both, suited to Central African conditions. But large-scale mechanization, or policies based on abstract principles, will not by themselves create them, nor show how they can be brought to life.

ESSAY IX

SOME REFLECTIONS ON CIVILIZATION IN AFRICA

I. INTRODUCTION

WHEN I was invited to deliver this Hoernlé Memorial Lecture, I regarded the invitation not only as a great privilege but as a duty. Like my friend, the late Jan H. Hofmeyr, who gave the first of these lectures, I felt under the constraint of *pietas* to accept the invitation. Hoernlé's work, friendship and personality greatly influenced me—although, I regret, I was not formally a pupil of his—from my earliest student days at this University, as well as later when I was privileged to be his colleague. Unfortunately, my visit to my *Alma Mater* is on this occasion all too brief, and I have had little time in which to attempt to do justice—even if I could do so adequately—to the memory of one of the greatest pioneers of racial understanding that South Africa has had the privilege of attracting to her shores.

It is only a few years ago that Jan H. Hofmeyr said in this hall that middle-age had crept suddenly upon him. Little did I realize that it would not be long before I would stand here to pay tribute to the memory of our mutual guide whose life inspired and continues to inspire all of us. For Hoernlé was not just 'in' South Africa ; he was part of all of it. Yet his world stretched far across all mundane boundaries, whether of race, religion, politics or nationality. He dedicated his philosophical thinking to the world, and his practical work to Africa—to Africa as a whole : Africa as part of the modern world. He was an idealist and always remained one. I remember another idealist : Sidney Webb, by then Lord Passfield, giving an address at a re-union dinner at the London School of Economics and Political Science. The chairman in introducing him expressed the hope that Lord Passfield was still the same idealist as Sidney Webb the student. To this Lord Passfield replied that life had taught him that to be half as idealistic at fifty is equivalent to being twice as idealistic as one had been at twenty-five. Hoernlé might well have said the same about himself. His faith in the power of human reason and co-operation was never dimmed, notwithstanding the disappointments that much of his non-academic work inevitably involved.

II. THE FALLACY OF 'FINAL' SOLUTIONS

True to the spirit of the thinker in whose memory this lecture is being given, I propose this evening to address my remarks not to those in search of ready-made solutions to social problems, but to those who, as students, seek for understanding and are prepared to devote time to contemplation in a spirit of calm and humble detachment. Only if that spirit is kept alive can any society hope to survive the dangers which threaten it from without, and the even greater dangers which so easily disrupt the very foundations of its being from within.

I have referred to ready-made solutions. Perhaps it will be as well for me to say that in so doing I was not thinking merely of the slogans which so easily take the place of political wisdom in the hectic modern world. What I had in mind was something more fundamental. The very idea of finding final ' solutions ' to social problems is the peculiar result of applying to the life of societies and individuals a category of thought which does not fit. We cannot speak of individuals or societies finally ' solving ' the problems which constitute the very essence of their being. Such ' solutions ' would pre-suppose an omniscience with which only gods, and not men, are endowed ; it would be necessary to assume that the problems involved were, like mathematical equations or logical constructs, capable of final solution : that solutions to social problems are inherent in a given set of premises. But in the problems of life and of living societies there are no given or clear-cut premises—other than the wide limits set by heredity and environment—and these are themselves subject to the influence of change.

It is this false analogy with mechanics and mathematics that accounts for the facile belief that the problem involved in living and working together in a community is similar to the problem of finding, by abstract thought or logical deduction, the ' unknown ' factor in an equation. In the realm of organic life there is, and can be, no final solution—other than death itself. What appears to be a ' solution ' at one moment of time is but the stage-setting for the problems of the next succeeding instant or, if you prefer, of the next turn of the cycle in the life process itself. Those who arrogantly write solutions upon their political banners, like the tyrants who promise to solve the problems of society for a thousand years to come, offend not only the gods, who in anger soon take vengeance upon them with thunderbolts of fire—they offend the very nature of all social evolution which rests on the slow unfolding of institutions, laws, and habit-patterns of thought and action.

III. The 'Catastrophic' View of History

Closely related to the mechanistic concepts which are inapplicable to the life of societies is that ' catastrophic ' or deterministic view of social processes which regards all history as a straight line : whether rising or falling, it is held in the vice-like grip of the unvarying determinants in accordance with which it is plotted by destiny itself—only a catastrophe can alter its direction. To minds benumbed by such symbolism history is a series of sudden eruptions which wipe the slate clean so that society can begin again with a different formula.

I was reminded recently of an example of this type of thinking when I had the good fortune to listen to a reading from Charles Dickens by that masterful actor Emlyn Williams. He read a passage from *A Tale of Two Cities*. I hope no one will think that, in reading a summary of it here, I am trying to emulate that great actor.

' Monseigneur, one of the great lords in power at the court held his fortnightly reception in his grand hotel in Paris. Monseigneur was in his inner room, his sanctuary of sanctuaries, the Holiest of Holies to the crowd of worshippers in the suite of rooms without. Monseigneur was about to take his chocolate. Monseigneur could swallow a great many things with ease, and was by some few sullen minds supposed to be rather rapidly swallowing France ; but his morning's chocolate could not so much as get into the throat of Monseigneur without the aid of four strong men besides the Cook ... Deep would have been the blot upon his escutcheon if his chocolate had been ignobly waited on by only three men ; he must have died of two. . . .

Monseigneur had one truly noble idea of general public business, which was, to let everything go on in its own way ; of particular public business, Monseigneur had the other truly noble idea that it must all go his way—tend to his own power and pocket . . . .

Yet, Monseigneur had slowly found that vulgar embarrassments crept into his affairs, both private and public, . . . For, the rooms though . . . adorned with every device of decoration . . . were, in truth, not a sound business ; considered with any reference to the scarecrows in the rags and nightcaps elsewhere, . . . they would have been an exceedingly uncomfortable business—if that could have been anybody's business ! . . .

But, the comfort was, that all the company at the grand hotel of Monseigneur were perfectly dressed. If the Day of Judgement had only been ascertained to be a dress day, everybody there would have been eternally correct. Such frizzling—and powdering and sticking up of hair, such delicate complexions artificially preserved and amended, such gallant swords to look at, and such delicate honour to the sense of smell, would surely keep anything going, for ever and ever. . . .

Everybody was dressed for a Fancy Ball that was never to leave off. From the Palace of the Tuileries, through Monseigneur and the whole Court, through the Chambers, the Tribunals of Justice, and all society (except the scarecrows), the Fancy Ball descended to the Common Executioner : who, in pursuance of the charm, was required to officiate ' frizzled, powdered, in a gold-laced coat, pumps, and white silk stockings '. . . And who among the company at Monseigneur's reception in that seventeen hundred and eightieth year of our Lord, could possibly doubt, that a system rooted in a frizzled hangman, powdered, gold-laced, pumped, and white-silk stockinged, would see the very stars out ! . . .

The show being over. . . . With a wild rattle and clatter, ... (Monseigneur's) carriage dashed through streets . . . with women screaming before it, and men clutching each other and . . . children out of its way. At last, swooping at a street corner by a fountain, one of its wheels came to a sickening little jolt, . . . and the horses reared and plunged.

But for the latter inconvenience, the carriage probably would not have stopped ;

A tall man in a nightcap had caught up a bundle from among the feet of the horses, and had laid it on the basement of the fountain, and was down in the mud and wet, howling over it like a wild animal.

' Pardon, Monsieur the Marquis ! ' said a ragged and submissive man, ' it is a child.'

' Why does he make that abominable noise? Is it his child? '

' Excuse me, Monsieur the Marquis—it is a pity—yes.'

. . . the tall man suddenly got up from the ground, and came running at the carriage . . . .

' Killed ! ' shrieked the man, in wild desperation. . . . ' Dead.'

The people closed around. . . . There was nothing revealed by the many eyes . . . but watchfulness . . . there was no visible menacing or anger . . . Monsieur the Marquis ran his eyes over them all, as if they had been mere rats come out of their holes. He took out his purse . . . 'See! Give him that.' He threw out a gold coin for the valet to pick up, and all the heads craned forward . . . as it fell. The tall man called out again with a most unearthly cry, ' Dead ! '

Monsieur the Marquis . . . was just being driven away with the air of a gentleman who had accidentally broken some common thing, and had paid for it, and could afford to pay for it, when his ease was suddenly disturbed by a coin flying into his carriage, and ringing on the floor.

' Hold ! ' said Monsieur the Marquis. ' Hold the horses ! Who threw that ? '

He looked to the spot . . . the wretched father was grovelling on his face on the pavement . . . and the figure that stood beside him was the figure of a dark stout woman, knitting.

' You dogs,' said the Marquis, . . . ' I would ride over any of you very willingly, and exterminate you from the earth. . . .'

So cowed was their condition, and so long and hard their experience of what such a man could do to them, within the law and beyond it, that not a voice, or a hand, or even an eye was raised. Among the men, not one. But the women who stood knitting looked up steadily, and looked the Marquis in the face.

He was driven on, and other carriages came whirling by in quick succession ; the Minister, the State-Projector, the Farmer-General, the Doctor, the Lawyer, the Ecclesiastic, the Grand Opera, the Comedy, the whole Fancy Ball in a bright continuous flcw, came whirling by. The rats . . . remained looking on for hours ; soldiers and police often passing between them and the spectacle. . . . The father had long ago taken up his bundle and hidden himself away with it . . . the one woman who had stood conspicuous, knitting, still knitted with the steadfastness of Fate. The water of the fountain ran, the swift river ran, the day ran into evening, so much life in the city ran into death according to rule, time and tide waited for no man, the rats were sleeping close together in their dark holes again, the Fancy Ball was lighted up at supper, all things ran their course.'

What is it that grips us in this masterful drawing? It is the sense of doom, the picture of the inevitable catastrophe, to which this Fancy Ball of make-believe was leading, and, as it were, was bound to lead—until the knitting woman would sit with her sisters knitting immovably, patiently, while the heads rolled in the sand and the guillotine continued day after day to do the work which history had ordained.

Our and our parents' generation have had experience enough of such recurring catastrophes, revolts, and tyrannies ; each to have been the last to complete the very work of history itself—only once again to be confronted with yet another and greater tyranny stretching over half the world : based on the communist dialectic of inevitable revolution and war. No wonder that we are moved by the passage I have just read. Yet, however it grips us, it presents but a half-truth ; and a dangerous half-truth.

It is false precisely where it gives the intended impression that it is describing the inevitable flow of history ; but it is not a study of historical process at all. It does not tell us how the Fancy Ball of make-believe arose. It is a snapshot of a moment in history. It can be likened to a scene from a film ; but it does not analyse why the film had such a scene at all, how the story began, and what the social forces were that caused the actors to play their parts.

History is not the record of external fate or providence condemning man along an inevitable road to destiny. It is, on the contrary, the record of man's infinitely variable choices, and of his experiences on the long unforeseeable path which he must forever climb with his fellow-men in society. As Bergson put it long ago, it is only when we momentarily reach a halting-place, and look back, that the path we made appears clear and pre-determined. But it is we who hewed it through forest and over rock ; at each step there were other paths which we might have taken and which would have led to other resting-places. Nor is it true that the climber can at any stage obliterate the marks which his exertions and sufferings have left upon his soul ; any more than the gnarled oak, with the marks of many twists and turnings upon its bark, can re-capture the pristine straightness of its youthful greenery. For man in society, as for man the individual, there is no way of beginning again from the beginning ; the slate cannot be wiped clean. However much he may wish it to be otherwise, the problems and burdens of civilization will be the same to-morrow as they were yesterday and are to-day : The uncertain path will have to be hewn out afresh.

No abstractions, no mere generalization, no Acts of Parliament, no mere slogans—democracy, liberty, fraternity, the class war, or other fancy dress of speech, can remove the constant burden of human choice. Neither obstinate pride in the power of abstract reason, or of science, nor blind sacrifice to his chosen idols will suffice as beacons on man's way. For man is moved at least as much by habit and emotion as by reason : the deeds to which he is accustomed may influence him more in what he believes he can, and should, do, than all the philosophies.

But man's choices are never merely individual : he does not and cannot stand alone ; he is both in and outside of society. Indeed, he would not know how to choose at all were he to be completely isolated : the burden of fear, which choice would then involve, would crush his spirit ere he tried to exercise it unfettered, unguided, and unsupported by his fellow-men.

IV. CIVILIZATION AS SOCIAL CO-OPERATION

It is not my intention to-night to attempt to give you a precise, coherent, or original definition of civilization ; for that task I am supremely unqualified. My aim is only to start a discussion and to deal with some very limited aspects of my subject. And, perhaps, the most characteristic and, certainly, the most troublesome aspect of what we are discussing, arises when we consider this working together of man with his fellow-man in society.

Civilization, in its simplest aspect may, as Professor J. R. Strayer has suggested, be thought of as the ability of people in society to work together effectively. When civilizations are in decay and decline, something which previously made that co-operation effective has been, or is being, lost or cast away. Men have ceased to believe in effective co-operant social action : they are held in a vice of fear. They believe themselves powerless to arrest the cynical disillusionment which grips them. In desperation they seek shelter in the worship of strange gods and beliefs. They are moved to catastrophic actions—even to attempts to annihilate those whom previously they thought their helpers. What but yesterday would have seemed to them impossible now appears as a necessary though headlong jump into the dark abyss of fate itself.

One of the marks of civilization is the ability of people in society to work together effectively. You will note the relative character of these words. They imply that civilization is not indicated merely by the possession of something absolute or material : it does not consist in the possession of tools or mechanical aids, of aeroplanes, motor-cars, plumbing, or of technical know-how. It is not something which exists *in vacuo*—irrespective of time and place or of man's external environment. It cannot be discerned from the colour of a man's skin or deduced from the exploits of his ancestors : to have been civilized yesterday does not imply that one is civilized to-day. The conditions necessary for effectively working together in society change constantly. The field of social co-operation widens and narrows ; but men may not be able to recognize such changes ; or they may lack the aptitude or will to accommodate themselves to them. For example, in times when men were organized for the most part in nomadic tribes the effective area of co-operation was very limited. One's own tribe was not dependent on the way of life of other tribes ; one could be relatively highly civilized within the bosom of one's tribal beliefs and gods, and yet one could destroy a neighbouring people without undermining the minimum conditions of effective co-operation in one's own. Given, however, an increase of population throughout the field in which such separate societies operated—given the need for a settled agrarian and trading economy with the concomitant growth of cities, then the minimum conditions of civilization take on a different aspect. The *mores* and the way of life of such societies, with their desert raids, and roaming existence, are no longer adequate. New standards of civilization have to be evolved. The tribal gods themselves must give way to more universal deities ; their work is done : to continue to worship them is now a sign of barbarism not of civilization—an obstacle to the pre-requisites of civilized life itself. Civilization is never an absolute state of being ; it is a process—a becoming—a changing inheritance of aptitudes, habits, beliefs, and continuing social action without clear-cut beginnings and without certain ends. A civilization which is not in process of change, which can be grasped, defined, cut off and circumscribed, is a civilization which is not living but has been, or is being, frozen into death.

V. The 'Frozen' Society

The harrowing aspect of the passage from Dickens which I have read lies precisely in that it describes with deep psycho-

M

logical truth and insight a society which is so frozen. What we hear is not the throb of life but the rattle of death. We are made to feel that nothing the actors can now do—no knowledge of wrong turnings in the past, no strivings in the future, can save them or their successors from the impending tragedy. Indeed, we are made to feel that the tragedy is not only inevitable but deserved : as retribution and punishment for the hapless and helpless actors on the stage.

This feeling results from that a-historical and a-sociological outlook to which I have already drawn attention. Notwithstanding his deep humanitarian feelings and sympathies, Dickens, in the last resort, like so many of his contemporaries, was thinking not in political or sociological, but in abstract, moralistic terms.[1] Such a view tends to regard civilization as something given : as wholly ' good ' or wholly ' bad '— ' superior ' or ' inferior ', as the triumph of good over evil, not of man in society forming new relationships, and ever adapting himself anew to his environment and his fellow-men.

Western Civilization has paid dearly with the blood and tears of millions because of the facile belief that civilization is not a process of trial and error, of continuous adaptation, of sympathy, and of slowly evolving mutual understanding, but merely a question of abstractions : of liquidating those who being bad, or rich, or different, must be swept away to make ' civilization ' possible. Time and again those who thought themselves the ' good ', the ' chosen ', the ' élite ', or, as divinely appointed emperors or tyrants, made the same but obverse mistake of regarding civilization as dependent only on them, or on their abstract concepts of perfection : oblivious to the changing exigencies of time and circumstance, regarding their estate and function as unalterable as the laws of the Medes and Persians ; despising both the opportunities for wider co-operation which the time enjoined, and the peoples whose power of co-operation it was necessary to seek, to cherish and to develop.

The frightening truth of Dickens's sketch lies, I have suggested, on the psychological plain. Here we see a society

---

[1] Cf. Eric Auerbach's valuable analysis of literature as a mirror of concepts of reality in his Mimesis : *Dargestellte Wirklichkeit in der Abendländischen Literatur. Eine Geschichte des Abendländischen Realismus als Ausdruck der Wandlungen in der Selbstanschauung des Menschen.* A. Francke AG. Verlag, Bern.

which has ceased to function because those in it have ceased to be aware of the minimum conditions for effective social action. The eyes, alike of Monseigneur, of the knitting woman, and of the miserable rats who line the road, only stare : nothing focuses them on a single common element of experience.

VI. The Need for Awareness

One of the fundamental pre-requisites of the process of civilization, I submit, is a certain state of awareness suited to the environment and passing circumstances in which men in society find themselves. It is an aptitude and not only a matter of social will: it rests on habit patterns of thought, perception, and action ; it involves the ability to take account of an ever-widening circle of needs ; of feeling and experiencing the relations and interdependence of the needs of the self and the needs of others. It is a form of loyalty—of loyalty, as J. H. Hofmeyr was ever at pains to emphasize, to an ever-widening circle of persons and institutions : to one's school, one's university, one's profession, one's village, one's city, one's province, one's state, and to the Commonwealth of States. It is the perception of reality as an expanding horizon of relations. It is this awareness of the nature of the human and natural surround, in which he has his being, that distinguishes the more from the less civilized man. As Professor Josef Pieper has recently written :[1]—

'Every living thing lives in a world, in " its " world, and " has " a world in which it lives. To live means to be " in " the world . . A stone . . . is not really related to the world " in " which it is, nor to the things " next to " which it lies, nor to those " with " which it is in the world. A relationship in the proper sense of the word, is a link established from inside to something external ; relations can only exist where there is an " inside " where there is a dynamic centre from which all activity proceeds . . . inwardness is the capacity to establish relations and to communicate . . . Only a being capable of having relations . . . has a world. Only a living being exists within a range of relationships. The world is a field of relations . . . the higher the *order* of a being, the more embracing and wider its power of establishing relations . . . the higher a being stands in the order of reality, . . . the wider and deeper its world.

---

[1] I am grateful to the publishers, Messrs. Faber and Faber, Ltd., for permission to quote this passage from Professor Josef Pieper's book : *Leisure the Basis of Culture* (London, 1952), p. 109 ff.

'The lowest world, the first step in the hierarchy, is that of a plant which does not extend its spatial world beyond the sphere of touch. . . . The animal's capacity to establish relations is greater is so far as it is capable of being sensibly and sensually aware ; " to be aware " of a thing is an entirely new mode of relating itself to a thing, unknown in the plant world. . . .'

But, and here we come to the analogy to which I am particularly anxious to draw your attention :

'It is by no means true . . . that everything an animal is able, abstractly speaking, to see or to hear, belongs to its " world " ; animals possessed of eyes do not actually see, nor could they see, everything that is visible in their " surroundings ". And surroundings . . . do not constitute a " world ".'

Contrary to the view that all animals with eyes saw the same object, Jacob von Uexkull, the biologist, whom Professor Pieper quotes, (p. 111), wrote :

'The animal's " environment " is something altogether different from the natural scene ; it more nearly resembles a small, poorly furnished room. . . . A jackdaw is utterly unable to see a grasshopper that is not moving. . . . We are perhaps inclined to suppose that although the shape of a grasshopper is familiar to the jackdaw, it is unable to recognize a grasshopper if a blade of grass cuts across it, it cannot recognize it as the " unity " grasshopper—just as we find it quite difficult to recognize a familiar object in a picture-puzzle. On this assumption it is only when the grasshopper jumps that its shape becomes recognizable and dissociates itself from the surrounding images. But further experiments lead one to suppose that a jackdaw simply does not know the shape of a motionless grasshopper and is so constituted that it can only apprehend the moving form. That would explain why so many insects feign death. If their motionless form simply does not exist in the field of vision of their enemies, then by shamming death they drop out of that world with absolute certainty and cannot be found even though searched for.'

'Animals are perfectly adapted,' concludes Professor Pieper, ' to their sharply defined and delimited environment—perfectly adapted to it, but equally, imprisoned within it, so that they cannot overstep the frontier in any way whatsoever : they cannot even find an object though armed with senses that are apparently well adapted to the purpose, unless, that is, the object fits completely into their selected, partial world.'

The analogy which I wish to press home is that, like animals, human beings may have eyes but see not, and ears but hear not. They may be imprisoned in a partial world : a world of illusion, penned in by myths and beliefs of the past, unable to scale the walls and look fearlessly upon the world— the larger world—of reality ; incapable of forming new relations with it, and their fellow-beings within it. But the establishment of such relations is, as I have said, not only a question of will. The sensitivity of awareness is formed only by practice. Civilization in process is this necessarily slow evolution through social action itself; to bar such evolution is to court its final breakdown.

VII. AFRICA: ILLUSION AND REALITY

Against this background I propose now to attempt to indicate some few of the vast changes in the human and non-human surround which have taken place in Africa in little more than half a century—even in little more than the lifetime of many in this hall to-night. They may serve to show—even if inadequately—the tasks which confront all the inhabitants of Africa in the problem of building a viable system of co-operation in the changing and dangerous times in which we live. In doing so I am conscious not only of the complexity of the issues involved but of my own shortcomings in attempting even to raise them. I raise them not because I am able to give ready answers to them, but because I feel it important that we should direct our minds to the deeper issues which are obscured by current slogans and ideologies.

The exploration of most of Africa south of the Sahara ; its partitioning among the Great Powers ; its linking to the modern world economy ; its gradual opening up by a network of communications—still inadequate to its needs—had its greatest momentum during that unique period in history, which has been described as ' the noon of a halcyon day of Victorian England which was fatuously expected to endure to eternity '.[1] The long diplomatic and military struggles of the great European Powers, which led finally to the establishment of their hegemony in Africa, are at an end ; so is the nearly three century long thrust of Europe into large parts of Asia. The optimism of nineteenth century Europe as the carrier of a finally perfected civilization available for export to all climes and continents has evaporated ; so too has the belief in nationalism as the necessary and sole vehicle of liberty : the self-determination of nations has been found—like patriotism

---

[1] L. B. Namier : *Avenues of History*, loc. cit.

—to be not enough. From the ruins of two generations of war there has arisen a striving for a new approach to the problems of Western civilization in an age where to stand alone—economically, politically, technically or culturally— is to court disaster. The easy generalizations of the nineteenth and early twentieth centuries have been tested and have been found wanting. To-day there is a searching, a questioning, a criticizing of concepts : nationality, sovereignty, imperialism, security, and the like, unparalleled in modern times. These questionings will bear fruit : in new alignments, institutions and new creative endeavour. The free world is painfully, but with vigour, forging new bonds of security and patterns of co-operative endeavour across national frontiers. Whatever its travail may produce, it will not produce a society dominated by a merely European outlook but a community increasingly conscious of the needs and aspirations of other peoples. Never before in history has there been such international concern and organized endeavour to discover new ways of international co-operation, on the basis of technical, economic, and sociological study, to combat want and political immaturity. The great advances and bold experimentation in British Colonial policies in Africa in recent years provide a striking illustration of this trend. The reasons for this revolution in Western thinking are many ; I cannot attempt to deal with them now. Apart, however, from the humanitarian drive behind them there is one which particularly concerns us here. It is the realization that in the jet and atomic age the free world is so closely interdependent for its security that the development of its resources on a trans-national scale has become a first priority for survival of the basic institutions on which its freedom rests.

It is against this common need that African policies will, I believe, come increasingly to be judged by those who will make the crucial decisions in the newly emerging power-constellations of the free world. In so far as pressure will be exerted on Africa it is not likely to arise, as in the past, from the power-politics of Europe. The dangers which threaten civilization in Africa come, in the first instance, not from without but from within ; from possible internal stresses and weaknesses. It is these which could once again throw Africa

—that half-way house between East and West—into the maelstrom of extra-African political struggles : a half-way house can only too easily become a battlefield.

It is well to remember that the continental peace from Cape to Cairo, which is so readily taken for granted, is a very recent, and, as yet, a very fragile thing. Before the early years of this century Africa was a continent of continuous bloody, tribal conflict, of slave raids, of frontier and colonial wars, and of the first large-scale war by Europeans in Africa against a European world power. The modern internal history of Africa is not the history of a peaceful continent but of a continent that, except for a very brief space of time, has known neither peace nor good government. Africa is not a politically mature but a politically immature continent : by far the greater part of its indigenous population has so far had little opportunity of gaining experience and developing the aptitudes and institutions for handling unaided many of the internal, and most of the inter-continental and foreign issues of government. The capacity for government, however, is not something that can be either merely taught, merely learned, or merely formulated and bestowed : it can only grow, and slowly evolve through the hard experience of social action and increasing responsibility ; and for its evolution peace and order are the primary requisites.

I suggest, therefore, that the most vital task, at the present time, for all the inhabitants of Africa, is to guard the peace of Africa, and, in particular, to eschew policies and dissensions which might have the consequences of again making this continent the cockpit of international rivalries. It would be calamitous for all the inhabitants of Africa if the unique period of inter-continental peace, which has so accidentally come about, should prove to have been but an Indian Summer. Perhaps at no previous time in modern history has the urgency been greater in Africa for calm deliberation and leadership designed to evolve continental co-operant political and economic institutions suited to the human and ecological environment of Africa itself.

In order that all the inhabitants of Africa should be able to take full measure of these heavy responsibilities, it is necessary that they should see this continent in terms of reality and not of illusion. It is equally necessary for those outside Africa, but with interests in it, to do so. Fifty years ago the spanning of Africa from Cape to Cairo and from East to West by a network of communications, and a system of modern law and order, was little more than a dream—an aspiration. To-day, notwithstanding the fact that, as Alan Paton has so picturesquely phrased it : ' if one were to journey over the Continent of Africa by plane, one would rarely by day see a moving vehicle on the ground. By night one would rarely see a light ', there are very few regions in Africa which have not already been in some way, directly or indirectly, linked to the outside world. There is no longer a single economic, political or cultural development anywhere in Africa, the far-flung ripples of whose effects, like the beats of the African drum, do not spread across the length and breadth of this continent : characterized as it is now by no natural barriers of any consequence from the Kalahari to the Sahara. Everything is in process of transition from the social and economic structures of pre-history through all stages of complexity up to the very heights of de-personalized, functionally organized, abstract metropolitan life in a city like Johannesburg—comparable as it is to that in any of the great financial and commercial centres of the world. Men and women from hundreds of tribes ; from a score of nations ; from many races and religions traverse the continent from North to South ; from East to West ; on foot, on horseback, on bicycles, in motor-cars, by air and by sea around its coasts. Everywhere the pattern of life is multi-racial, multi-tribal and multi-national. The pattern of life in Africa is not standardized or streamlined : it is not that of either Europe or Asia. Many races have sojourned in it, influenced it, or been absorbed by it ; but none have yet left an indelible mark upon it. It is this continent, of many hues and colours, of all stages of civilization—a continent so old and yet so young—which *is* Africa : the Africa which throws its fascinating spell over all those whose awareness to reality has not been dulled; the Africa which stimulated the explorers, the missionaries, and scientists, the great British, French, Belgian and Dutch colonial administrators, the traders, the prospectors, miners, engineers, the pioneers, the voortrekkers, the settlers and the money-makers to unravel the secrets it so long held locked in a somnambulant past—when life for most of its peoples, beset with the dangers of a cruel environment, was generally ' nasty, brutish, and short '. This Africa is indeed a continent with a life, a reality, and a spirit of its own—if we would but pause to catch its rhythm—drowned as it all too often is, by the tumult of the modern world ; by the lack of patience of those greedy for immediate gain, and by ignorance of those unaware of the pace of Africa. For Africa has also a tempo of its own ; those who would build a supple, living, all-embracing civilization in this continent must hasten slowly and realize that the way is long, through parched land and thick scrub ; and that guidance from the past is hard to come by, and cannot be read by those who run, but must be unearthed patiently : not only with the aid of the physical but also of the human sciences.

I have another purpose in painting these aspects of African realities. It is to draw your attention to the fact that the very enthusiasm and rapidity with which the present super-structure of mechanical civilization has been erected in Africa has left us little time for awareness of the changing human foundations on which it rests. It is usual for the inhabitants of Africa to regard these problems as unique ; but the problems of human relations are nowhere unique in relation to the passions and emotions, the hopes, the fears and the rationalizations which men invent to hide them from themselves. If it were otherwise history would be a meaningless tale told by an idiot.

VIII. Africa : The Basis of Human Relations

It is, I know, rash to endeavour to characterize great historical movements in general terms or phrases. Yet, reluctantly, I must, owing to the brief time available to me, make use of this device. If I were asked what have been the two poles about which the human forces in Africa have played with the greatest tension, I would say land and status ; both for African and non-Africans these and little else have in the past spelled the security which they have sought and still seek. Security for the indigenous inhabitants of the continent has meant, and over vast areas still means, possession of land

and the desire to live within the security of the particularistic, custom-bound, status-regulated bosom of tribal life and institutions. To the white pioneers in South Africa land and certainty of status with the freedom and security they gave, was what they sought. But, be it noted, they fought for a particular kind of freedom—a freedom *from* what they wished to escape : freedom to live their own lives on far-flung lands, with their own servants and their own herds, in almost patriarchal simplicity ; freedom to live a life mainly regulated, not by the universalistic rules of the market, nor by the money-mechanism, but founded on hierarchical relationships and on *pietas*—to which my friend and teacher, Professor Haarhoff, has so often drawn attention.

All social relationships postulate a basis on which membership in the relationship shall be built. Thus the basis of relations between a doctor and patient, a tribal chief and his people, a bywoner and the relative who has given him land to utilize in exchange for part-time service on his master's farm, all differ from the criteria of relationship which, for example, govern a wage contract in an urban factory, or the relationship of a bank to its customers. The following definition from an important contemporary study sums up the distinctions here involved :—

' The membership criteria for a relationship will be called *universalistic* if persons are chosen for it or admitted to it on the basis of criteria that satisfy two conditions : (1) that they be criteria such that no individual is barred by social structures from possessing or acquiring them, and (2) that they be criteria such that they are germane to the purpose for which selection is made. The membership criteria for a relationship will be called more or less *particularistic* to the degree and in the respect that any departure whatever is made from the two conditions set up in the definition of *universalistic* '[1]

---

[1] Cf. Marion J. Levy, Jr. *The Structure of Society*, to whose work I am greatly indebted. Cf. also his (with Shih Kuo-Heng) *The Rise of the Modern Chinese Business Class*. (Institute of Pacific Relations, New York, 1949). I am also indebted to the work of Professor Talcott Parsons, particularly his *Theory of Social Action*. Of the distinction between universalistic and particularistic criteria Levy quotes the following relevant passage from Parsons : ' Like all such analytical distinctions it does not preclude that both elements may be involved in the same concrete situation. But nevertheless their relative predominance is a matter of the greatest importance.' Selection criteria that tend to minimize but do not entirely eliminate particularistic elements will be called *predominantly universalistic*. Those that tend to minimize but do not entirely eliminate universalistic elements will be called predominantly *particularistic*. (Parsons : *The Professions and Social Structure Essays*, p. 192).

What I am particularly concerned with here are the occupational and economic implications of these social relationships. In the occupational sphere[1] ' the criteria for selection are more nearly universalistic the more they are concerned with *what a person can do that is relevant to the job*, and they are more particularistic the more they are concerned with *who he is regardless of the relevance of his identification to the job*.'

If an employer, for example, is by law or custom permitted only to employ persons of one race, and not another, he is forced to emphasize a particularistic element in the employer-employee relationship which is clearly not related to the efficiency of the work which the employee is required to do, and which the efficient conduct of the business or industry postulates. Similarly, if one class, or race of persons is not given access to land or property, and is prohibited from exercising its aptitudes or potential aptitudes in putting such resources to use, then a particularistic element is interfering with the economic, or potential economic efficiency of the society.

In different societies the basis of social relationships is subject to very wide variations and a society resting on purely universalistic relations would suffer intolerable stresses. The real point of importance, however, is that in order to survive every society must be aware of the extent to which it can, under altered circumstances, permit itself the luxury of retaining criteria for social relations which run counter to the reality of its changing needs, and to the exigencies of the wider world of which it is a part. If a society were to continue to insist on outmoded criteria then in altered circumstances it could not long survive. For example, in a society where there are rules permitting only women to work in the fields, while the men are enjoined to hunt, continued insistence on such criteria in the face of new kinds of work necessitated by the growth of population, the need for modern agriculture, and, of course, by the disappearance of the wild game would completely undermine the existence of the community.

The social and economic history of large parts of Africa— particularly of the Union—in the last fifty years can be summed up by the rate at which the predominantly particularistic

[1] Ibid., p. 251.

societies—both European and non-European—have been destroyed, or are, as in the rest of Africa, in process of dis-integration. Of course, all the well-known economic indices illustrate this thesis : to see is, however, not necessarily to recognize. Like individuals, societies often retain a mental picture of what they think they look like (usually a flatteringly younger picture) even when they daily look at their changed reflection in the mirror. Indeed, psychologists have reported a pathetic case in which an elderly woman obstinately main-tained that the person she saw when looking into the mirror was her younger sister and not herself.

I can think of no better way of bringing home the difference between the younger sister—now long-deceased—who was South Africa, and whose image still so frequently be-devils the thinking of the older, living sister—than by examining some statistics of population. These indicate, perhaps most unambiguously, how tremendous have been the changes which separate Africa to-day from that Africa of the past in which Europeans could go on living side by side with the indigenous peoples without the conscious emergence of any common world of relations between them.

IX. POPULATION CHANGES[1]

Let me first draw your attention to the significant fact that at the time when, roughly speaking, the modern economy of South Africa had begun to be developed in earnest—say about 1891—there was a total population of all races of about 4.1 million[2] in the whole of South Africa. Yet to-day it is prob-

---

[1] In selecting the figures given in this section I have done so with the purpose only of making very broad contrasts. The figures of urbanization are subject to very great qualifications as they have unavoidably been amended from time to time according to different definitions of what communities are covered by the term ' urban '. For the statistics of ' urbanization ' for years prior to 1946 I have relied on Dr. Shannon's article. It must also be borne in mind that figures for population in territories other than the Union, even for recent years, leave very much to be desired. I should particu-larly like to stress that anybody making use of the figures should first consult the valuable article by Dr. H. A. Shannon on Urbanization, *1904–1936* in the *South African Journal of Economics* for 1937 Vol. 5, page 164. The article, to which I am greatly indebted, discusses fully the different definitions of urbanization and analyses the statistical methods adopted by the different censuses in the Union and its constituent Provinces.

[2] The number of 4.1 million probably overstates the position, as I have had to use the figures for 1904 for Natal and the Transvaal. In any case the figures for earlier dates for Natal do not include Zululand—which was included for the first time in the census of 1904.

able that a number very nearly equal to that whole population of 60 years ago is living in towns in the Union of more than two thousand European inhabitants.[1] According to the 1946 census the number at that date was 3.6 million.

Incidentally, it is worth remarking that in 1865—the hey-day of the youth of the deceased younger sister of present-day South Africa—the total European population of the then most populous province, the Cape Colony, was only 180,000 —about four-fifths of the European population of Cape Town to-day ; and even the total European population of the Orange Free State and the Transvaal together in 1891 was only 196,000—less than the number of Europeans (about 220,000) in Cape Town in 1946.

It is also worth noting that the European population of the whole of Natal in 1891 was only about 47,000—considerably less than that of Germiston in 1946. Indeed, in 1946, the fifteen largest towns in the Union, with a population exceeding 20,000 Europeans each, had a total European population which exceeded the number of Europeans in the whole of South Africa in 1904. (The figures were 1,182,000 as compared with 1,117,000). Actually, the number of Africans in the city and suburbs of Johannesburg alone in 1946 (387,175) greatly exceeded all the Africans in urban centres in the whole of the Union in 1904, when the total urbanized African population was about 243,000, and formed roughly 7 per cent of the total African population of the Union (3.5 million). By 1921 the corresponding percentage was 9 ; by 1936 it was 14, and in 1946 it was 20 (the figures for 1946 were : African urbanized 1.5 million ; total African population 7.8 million). The number of Europeans in urban centres, as defined above, in 1904 was roughly 40 per cent of the total

[1] It can, of course, be argued that towns containing two thousand Europeans are hardly a good index of urbanization in a country with such vast distances as the Union. Dr. Shannon has, I think rightly, drawn attention to this. I wish, however, to make it clear that I am not concerned with this point here—for my purposes these figures are quite adequate, as I am intending to show the destruction of a predominantly particularistic society. I should also like to draw attention to the important point that the Union censuses register persons according to the place where the census is held. In fact, however, in the Union the impact of ' urbanization ' is not fully indicated in this manner. A large number of non-Europeans, particularly Africans, are continually moving from their ' rural ' or ' tribal ' surroundings into towns for short periods, so that many more persons are affected by the more universalistic economy into which they are endeavouring to fit than are indicated by the census figures at any one moment of time.

European population of South Africa ; by 1946 it had risen to just over 60 per cent ; for all races the corresponding percentage had risen from 17 to roughly 32 and the total population of the country had more than *doubled* from 5.1 to 11.4 million. Finally, in regard to the Union, it is worth noting that the total population in 1951 at about 12.6 million has increased more than threefold since 1891.

The population trends to which I have drawn attention in the Union are indicative of what is happening in the rest of Africa at a slower rate. In 1900 the population of Accra in the Gold Coast was only about 16,000. It is now well over 130,000. Lagos Township had a population of about 41,000 in 1901. It now has a population of about 230,000, which, on the basis of the 1946 census, would have made it the third largest town in the Union. Incidentally, Ibadan now has a population of about 335,000 ; this is greater than the total European population of Johannesburg. In 1906 there were 559 Europeans in Nairobi, and the whole population was 11,612. In 1948 there were over 10,000 Europeans, over 43,000 Asiatics and over 75,000 Africans, a total of 129,000 in the city ; this would have made it the seventh largest town in the Union on the basis of the 1946 census. In 1951 the total European population of Southern Rhodesia was 136,000, of which over 72,000 lived in Salisbury, and Bulawayo and their suburbs ; these two towns, with their districts, accounted for a labour force of nearly 180,000 Africans.

The figures for the Union, I suggest, provide a striking delineation of some of the features which distinguish the real South Africa from that illusory sister-image to which I have referred. For what these figures mean is that if, by a wave of a wand, it were possible for the inhabitants of South Africa to be moved back in time to the separate feudal and tribal ' worlds ' of the ' golden ' past most of the present population of South Africa would starve at once. It is only because by far the largest part of the population now works and lives, either in whole or in part, within a modern economy closely linked to, and very greatly dependent upon, world markets that the existing population of South Africa can maintain even its present average low standards of living. But, as everyone knows, the largest part of the work by which the Union's population manages to attain even these low standards is conducted on the basis of criteria which are not at all relevant to the effectiveness of its work, but are based on laws and customs which contribute nothing to that effectiveness, but, on the contrary, greatly undermine it. It is to this fact, and mainly to this fact, that South Africa must ascribe its relative poverty and the obvious stresses and strains in the body-politic which arise therefrom.

This is a very common phenomenon. Over large parts of the world the so-called pressure of population on food supplies does not result merely from the scarcity of ' natural ' resources but rather from ignorance, and from habits, customs, laws and institutions which for one reason or another prevent available resources from being utilized or further developed.

There is urgent need for a continent-wide study of these questions in Africa. Contrary to expectations, the development of agricultural resources does not appear to be keeping pace with the growth of population. Even the output of many of the raw materials, which form the basis of Africa's agricultural exports, appears to show a disappointing rate of growth in comparison with the other raw-material producing regions of the world. Unless the work of the inhabitants of Africa as a whole in relation to the difficult environment of the continent, can be made more effective by the necessary changes in existing habit patterns of social action, the outlook for the future is disturbing. All over Africa the increasing numbers can no longer be adequately provided for on the basis of the methods, the institutions or the particularistic, functionally diffuse and hierarchical relationships of the past ; yet, on the basis of the changes in these which the times demand there is no foreseeable limit to the expansion of population and productivity in this, as yet, so undeveloped continent.

X. The Dangers of Uprootedness

The great industrial and mining developments in Africa have drained, and continue to drain, the countryside of its able-bodied population ; but they have not provided, and continue to do little to provide an economically meaningful and socially stable way of life. A population can adopt criteria

of relationships suited to either an 'urban-industrial' or
'rural-agricultural' way of life just as, to use a different
analogy, it can adapt itself to predominantly universalistic or
predominantly particularistic criteria—although the latter are
not suited to a modern industrial economy; but it is not
possible to ensure any stability in a society which hovers in a
twilight of social existence, which cannot find a basis for
any permanent relationship at all. It is quite possible to achieve
an increase in all the usual economic indices of productivity,
and yet fail to safeguard the very foundations of a stable
society.

Thus urbanization in South Africa, and a similar trend in
other parts of the continent, carries with it great dangers. The
whole question demands the most painstaking impartial
investigation by social scientists. For the present rate of
urbanization indicates the presence of what is, perhaps, the
most baffling of modern social diseases—mass uprootedness :
men and women torn, too rapidly, from the soil, the *mores*,
the loyalties, the obediences, and the sanctions to which they
were accustomed, and which they could understand.

This is how one of the most eminent of modern historians
pictures the disease with which European civilization has
been infected by the growth of amorphous collectivities.
'For men rooted in the soil there is, as a rule', writes Professor Sir Lewis Namier,[1] 'a hierarchy of allegiances : to
their village community or estate, to their district, to their
"country"—for them the nation is of a naturally federal
structure. Traditional beliefs and hereditary ties persist ; class
and the way of living determine alignments ; things are
individual and concrete in the village or the small, old-
fashioned town. But in the great modern cities men grow
anonymous, become ciphers, and regimented ; thinking
becomes more abstract and is forced into generalizations ;
inherited beliefs are shaken and old ties are broken ; there is a
void, uncertainty, and hidden fear which man tries to master
by rational thought. He starts by proudly asserting the rights
of the abstract average individual freed from the bondage of
tradition, and then integrates him into the crowd, a collective

---

[1] *Avenues of History*, Hamish Hamilton, London, 1952, 6, 26–27. I wish to thank
the publishers and author for permission to quote the above passage.

personality, which unloads itself in mass movements. The mass is the refuge of the uprooted individual ; and disintegration of spiritual values is as potent a process as the splitting of the atom ; it releases the demonic forces which burst all dams. The programme may be social revolution, or national revolution, or both ; the aim may be to right wrongs or to sweep away stultifying incumberances ; the result can be liberation, but it can hardly be liberty which is founded on restraint and not on force, even if genuine idealism guides it. "Whenever a single definite object is made the supreme end of the State", wrote Lord Acton, "be it the advantage of a class, the safety or the power of the country, or the support of any speculative idea, the State becomes for the time absolute. Liberty alone demands for its realization the limitation of the public authority . . ." Liberty is the fruit of slow growth in a stable society ; is based on respect for the rights of the individual, deeply embedded in the life and habits of the community ; is in its origin an aristocratic idea ; of the self-conscious individual, certain of himself and his position, and therefore perfectly at ease. It spreads when every man's house becomes "his castle" ; yet he must have a house and be safely rooted.'

The disease of uprootedness strikes everywhere in Africa without distinction of colour, race, or creed. Like cancer it is a silent disease : it kills when it is recognized too late. In Africa the fierce forces of Western industrialism are erecting a superstructure which is as dazzling as it is blind to the silent diseases which it carries with it. The basic problems of uprootedness in Africa are not unique, but the resistance of its peoples to its onward march is weaker than elsewhere— Africa lacks the defences provided in Europe by the gradual evolution from earlier associations, loyalties and social relationships : the sturdy peasant, the artisan disciplined by the craft-guild, the justice of the peace, the squire, and the long growth of local government and democratic institutions. The social soil of Africa is shallow : the roots of modern civilization cannot penetrate deep to resist the storms of circumstance ; the least disturbances, like the rain and the wind, create a dust-bowl and a desert.

As yet neither the indigenous nor the immigrant peoples

of the continent are sufficiently aware that civilization in process involves not only disintegration but conservation. In a larger sense that is also the basic problem of our time : to find a compromise between our aspirations on the one hand, and on the other hand our aptitudes—particularly our aptitudes to stand the stress of social change. In Africa there has as yet been insufficient realization and awareness of this crucial problem. Indeed, the problems involved in creating a civilization which can endure in Africa have so far been given little conscious attention. The modern history of Africa too often exhibits merely the desire of its various peoples to obtain freedom only in that limited sense in which it denotes freedom from something : freedom from some aspect of reality, from the exigencies of the world outside Africa, and from the inconvenience of realities in Africa. But real freedom is not thus negative. It cannot rest on the desire to escape from reality, from moral obligations, or from oneself ; the final expression of such degraded freedom is, as Berdyaef has written, ' leave me in peace '. Yet full creative freedom, and peace, in Africa can come to the extent, and only to the extent, that all the inhabitants in all parts of Africa accept the tasks which Africa imposes ; accept what Africa with all its diversities is ; accept the varying aptitudes, abilities and experiences of its different peoples ; and mutually respect their free personality and human dignity—without which there can be no freedom in any sense whatever.

I began this lecture by saying that there are no final solutions to social problems. There are only ways of continuously thinking and acting in relation to them. ' *Onbekend is onbemind.*' says an Afrikaans proverb ; yet true knowledge is not just a matter of intellectual appreciation : to know involves inspiration, illumination, sympathy and action. There is only one way of learning to play the flute, that is to play the flute. There is only one way of building a system of effective co-operation in society—building a civilization ; that is by building it—daily, wholly, unselfishly ; until to each one in his daily task the unaccustomed becomes the accustomed, and the way which was no way becomes a way : a path—a road—across the valleys and over the mountain tops.

It is an old recipe but it has not lost its efficiency, as I learned when a very 'modern' social psychologist told me in America recently : ' we have found an unfailing remedy for racial disharmonies—we get people to work together at a common task ; the task takes over and new illumination lightens up the scene.'